Outlive Me
Thirty Years of Poems and Writings

by ARNIE GOLDMAN

Copyright © 2005 by Arnie Goldman

ISBN 1-4196-1525-4
The Library of Congress Catalog Card Number: 2005908700

The text of this book is composed in Apollo.
Book design by Q Collective
Family photographs by Arnie Goldman

All proceeds from the sale of *Outlive Me* will be split between four charity organizations: The Susan G. Komen Breast Cancer Foundation (www.susangkomen.org), The Rainbow Connection (www.rainbowwishconnection.org), The Kenny Goldman Athletic Fund of the JCC Detroit (www.jccdet.org), and JARC (www.jarc.org).

For Kenny
my brother

"I guess I could be pretty pissed off about what happened to me, but it's hard to stay mad when there's so much beauty in the world. Sometimes I feel like I'm seeing it all at once and it's too much. My heart fills up like a balloon that's about to burst and then I remember to relax and stop trying to hold onto it and then it flows through me like rain and I can't feel anything but gratitude for every single moment of my stupid little life, you have no idea what I'm talking about, I'm sure, but don't worry, you will someday."

— LESTER BURNHAM (Kevin Spacey)
American Beauty, 1999

Contents

Intro and Acknowledgements xi

One Classroom

Classroom 2
Camouflage 4
Nightmare with Shoes 5
Yearbook 6
Hands 8
Thanksgiving 9
Hunger 10
Old Man Yellow 16
For You (on your 21st birthday) 17
The Recoil 18
A Bad Poem 19
Reflections on a New Year Casualty 20
pieces 21
Blurred Vision 22

Two Ghosts of the Fathers

After The Fact 32
Rings 33
Card-players 34
Waking in the Jewish Home for the Aged 36
On Your Birthday 38
The Echoes Of The Dead 39
Empty Chairs 40

Three Pass Away

Extranjero 44
Passing 46
Saturday Night, From a Chair on the Porch 47
Last Call 48
Blood-Breath 49

Snapshots 51
Lines 53
Pass Away 55
Mother 58
Echo 59
Twenty One 60

Four One Year Into Another

One Year 66
Wednesday 68
Kenny's Song 70
Severance 73
Breath 75
To the Goldmans 78
Forgetting My Uncle 82
Championships 85
Summer's Bookends 88

Five Anniversaries

Journal Pieces 1992-2002 94
In Memory of Kenny Goldman 101
the dead come crawling 103
Tumor 104
Tax Season 108
Apart 111
Anniversary Song 114

Six Permanent

My First Love 118
Crack 129
Burnout 132
Out of the Closet 134
Down 142
Groomsman 145
Outlive Me 149
Permanent 151
Namesake 154

Intro and Acknowledgements

Regret. When someone asks if you regret anything about your life, you're supposed to say no; I would do it the same way if I had to do it over again. At least that's what you hear on TV interviews.

Unlike all of the satisfied people, I've had lots of regrets. I regret how little I've written since college. I didn't have the guts to write much, I didn't seek any feedback, nor did I send anything away for publication. I've been a "closet writer," periodically writing a poem, article, story, speech, or eulogy and rarely letting anyone read or hear what I'd written.

I graduated from Wayne State University in Detroit, Michigan in 1979, a college I attended because I received a full scholarship, I was afraid to go away to school, and because my best friend also got a scholarship and decided to go to Wayne. When I was deciding what I wanted to do with my life, I looked at natural health, chiropractic, and medicine, being a full-fledged vegetarian health fanatic at the time. I hated pre-med classes and loved writing classes, so I suddenly made up my mind that I didn't know what I was going to be in life but I knew damn well I wasn't going to be a doctor. I wrote poetry and short stories and won the only writing contest I ever entered, the Tompkins Award at Wayne State. I graduated with a double major in English and Psychology and was a Merit Scholar and Phi Beta Kappa as well. In other words, I couldn't find a job. I stopped trying after walking out of the K Mart headquarters in 1979 and I never interviewed again. Instead, I stayed at my dad's business, Hardware Sales and Supply, where I had been working part time. I knew that one day I would get a "real job." Hardware Sales and Supply eventually became IDN-Hardware Sales, Inc. and in the years that followed I started caring about this company and its people. I wanted to help my father make the company better and so I stayed and eventually became its President. The company grew from seven people in 1979 to eighty-five people and ten locations today. But still, I ask myself, What am I going to do with my life?

What's the point of regret, because you can't go back and change anything. Still, there are real regrets. I regret that my best friend, Lewis Stone, didn't stop me in fifth grade from accidentally pounding Marty Adelman's head on the desk when the teacher was out, breaking his front tooth in half. Lewis, when he was in sixth grade, died in his sleep of a brain aneurism. I regret that I lived the cozy life and sacrificed my true passion, writing, to make a living purchasing and selling locks and security hardware in my father's business. I regret that I never tried to be a "real writer" because I never felt good enough to do it. I regret that I never got to meet my grandmother, Anna, whom I was named after and regret that she lived in a mental institution the last sixteen years of her life. I regret 9/11/2001, the day after my mother's sixty-sixth birthday. I regret the loss of so many I loved who died too early, like Aunt Shirley, my dad's youngest sister, who committed suicide in her bathroom in her Pacific Palisades home in California, and my cousin, Mike, my other Aunt Shirley's youngest son, who died mysteriously before he was 40, in his small suburban home. I regret that I sold the two Super Bowl tickets I'd been given in

1982 after a three hour icy car ride with my brother, Kenny, who was 13, (I was 25.) And how can I not regret the devastating night after a Detroit Tigers' baseball game on a hot July night seven months later when my father's car was blind-sided by another car and Kenny lived for only a few hours more, dying after midnight.

Twenty-three years later I realize I have many reasons to give thanks. I am thankful I am finally producing a book of writing, even if it is read by only family and friends. I am thankful for my parents, Milt and Rochelle, who let me be whatever I decided to be without pushing. They would have supported me whether I became a starving poet or a successful doctor or just an order picker at Hardware Sales. I am thankful to have worked alongside my father, whether yelling at each other or hugging, as long as I did. I am thankful for my gifted and loving sister, Leslie, and her dedicated husband, Bruce, and their wonderful daughter, Karenna. I am thankful for the few years I was blessed to have a brother like Kenny who inspired me with his humor, his love of fun and sports, and his friendship.

I am especially thankful for my wife, Judy, who saved me from myself in 1984, two years after Kenny died. She has given me so much over the years, which only she and I share. She and her parents and siblings have filled a lot of emptiness over the years. And she has been a loving mother to our three fantastic children, Kyle, Ilana, and Marlee, who have been amazing to watch as they've grown from little breathing bodies to the people they are today. I want to thank all of them for helping me to be the person I am and the writer that I want to be.

I want to donate all proceeds from this book to four charitable institutions:

The Susan G. Komen Breast Cancer Foundation, which for 20 years has been building awareness and raising $750 million for innovative breast cancer research and community outreach programs.

The Rainbow Connection, which is a Michigan non-profit organization established in 1985 that grants wishes to children, 3-18 years old, who have been diagnosed with life threatening diseases.

The Kenny Goldman Athletic Fund, established and named for my brother, which teaches children the spirit and techniques of basketball and allows kids to participate in a high quality basketball league.

And last but not least, JARC, which is a non-sectarian, community-based, Jewish residential service in Southeastern Michigan whose mission is to enable people with disabilities to lead full, rich lives.

I hope that readers will take away something meaningful from my book of poetry and writings, and that we can help raise needed funds for these important charitable organizations.

Arnie Goldman
2005

One
Classroom

Classroom
1976

Eighteen people in a circle,
low-pitched voices filtered
by the constant rumble, the hissing
of the heat—but it's still cold

in the streets out there,
beyond the chilled glass,
that market-stockyard planet
sitting, stuffed and slouching,

with darkened hands too stiff
to shake. And it's cold inside,
in this half-lit space
they call a classroom:

cracked-white walls surrounding us,
concrete slabs above our heads.
Withdrawn, almost patiently we sit,
await directions, maps that lead us

from one door to another, lecture
to test, distant voice to distant voice.
So we hide amongst the strangers
that we are. We tick in cadence

with the clock, slowly,
constantly, yet unaware of time.
The air drizzles down upon us
but we can hardly breathe

without fear, without useless
inhibitions. We talk in poems—
masquerades in rhymes, foreign words—
splices of silence in between,

afraid to lose ourselves
in each other's hands,
each impenetrable eye.
We choose to remain immune.

Camouflage
1976

The wind seethes. Its teeth
scratch the window like chalky fingers
on a door. A gray squirrel, its eyes
peering at me from the ledge,
squirms, searches the rocks for eyes,
and drops behind the shade.

The curtains whisper at me.
The shimmer dies before I speak.
As laughter to rain,
the camouflage is precise.

Only the wind sings,
Only the wind—a dull, fading laughtrack
Switched to rewind—
And only one listens.

A car is hurled past the window,
its faces indistinct, plastered
against the dull green metal,
a Polaroid snapshot.
A bicycle follows in slow motion,
Its wheels revolving like roulette wheels
That never stop at my number.

Nightmare With Shoes
1977

They've stared at me from my closet
off and on for the last so-and-so years,
their multiple eyes
and gaping mouths. If you look
closely, you'll see lines,
wrinkles written in brown ink
or foam-padded lips
stretched oblong beyond screaming;
how they lie mute, obsequious,
tongues shaved, teeth pulled,
making room for me.

My feet fit them nicely,
large slices of meat
inside their leather mouths,
blood-drained,
scraped from the pain of cows
into this long angular silence.

I string them up, gag them with socks,
150 pounds of tissue and blood.
If I knew before the meaning
of slaves, I would always go barefoot.

Now, I think they become me.

Yearbook
1977

The last page has three photos:
a clock, hourglass, and train.
They called it LIFE AND TIMES.
My mom made me buy it

before the Pomp and Circumstance,
cardboard diploma in my left hand.
It cost five dollars.
I couldn't care less.

It's funny now (like old westerns,)
those rollicking teens,
the good old days.
I didn't let anyone sign it.

Faces are signatures, I guess:
S as a child, with ballet skirt,
hands on hips, pigtails on both sides,
her clownish "Watch me!" laugh,

L., half-hearted, a snide look
at a friend; my teacher,
W. we called her, smiling.
Where did they go,

this veritable who's who,
my past smiling at me?
When I see L. at college,
older, more beautiful,

walk by me, it's not
nostalgia. Or S.
I wrote her months ago,
gave her some poems.

She never wrote back.
W? She left teaching
two years ago, haven't
seen her since.

But regret isn't it either,
or sadness or pain.
I look through every page
and can't forget

but want to.
S. bequeathed to "Wally and Barb,
beans and weenies."
I bequeathed nothing.

Hands
1977

Her hands, dark
and shivering, dart out
from sleeves, webbed

with little bones
and lines. Through the cold air
they'll skate, naked

swerve one minute, shift slightly
the next, touch and clasp
and break apart

like swirling birds.
When least expected,
they'll caress and slip away

into sleep, or slide gently
over my cheeks.
But on evenings like this,

strange and cold,
they'll hide between knees
or in denim-skinned pockets

afraid of me,
of this sultry warmth that burns
and scars.

Thanksgiving
1977

The way her skin peels off her breast,
Her dainty bones arched against the chest,
Her wings once spread so wide ripped apart,
The crest from the sky, the belly from the heart.

A transplant of bread replaces her blood
Once designed to flow. Now it knows
The final heart; lying in the white stove,
The flames expanding, parching the skin;
Once it goes, it goes.

Hunger
1977

PART I

I can't satisfy myself. What else in life is there but food, and who ever has enough? I was born in a woman who could not bear the thought of food wasted. She ate everything she could so I could live. She fed herself Ocean Spray Grapefruit Juice (vitamin C,) Carnation's Low Calorie Cocoa Mix with Marshmallows (calcium,) Pillsbury Butterflake Dinner Rolls (artificial Vitamin B6,) Mrs. Paul's Light Battered Fish and Chips (protein,) and Del Monte's Pineapple Chunks canned in heavy syrup (for her own sweet tooth.) She fed herself so I could live. She gave me everything she had in the world, and that was food. From her nipples poured the sweet scent of milk, from her hands came the spoon that fed me applesauce. She gave me her body so I could feed.

Now, when I make my monthly visit, she looks me in the gut and asks again, Do I live to eat or eat to live? I would assume the answer is obvious.

PART II

Tonight, the TV guide shows an interesting array of program selections. It doesn't matter. I sit with a pillow at the edge of the couch, approximately nine feet from the 19" Hitachi TV with remote control and digital clock. The remote control gives me all the power I've ever wanted, the power to adjust what I see, to turn Bing Crosby into a chipmunk, Mac Davis into darkness. But most importantly, it gives me time, saves me precious seconds. Not having to ascend from my nearly horizontal position on the couch to a vertical hunch so I can turn the dial from one station to another allows me just the few moments I need to make crucial decisions in the refrigerator: Mrs. Paul's Devilled Crab Miniatures or Green Giant's Green Peppers Stuffed with Beef and Crumbs? Nabisco's Crème Sandwich Cookie or Banquet's Frozen Banana Cream Pie? Decisions which have to be made in seconds and prepared in one to three minutes.

It's 6:30. I turn from the news to reruns of *Laverne and Shirley*. Laverne enters, applause. She yells to Shirley in the other room, "Shirl, where'd you put..." I turn to the nightly business report, stocks down, I turn back to the news. Poland's suffocating, two people were shot in the back of their station wagon on the northeast side of Detroit. No names disclosed, no clues. It's time to eat, I'm famished. I choose a quick soup, Campbell's Chunky Beef and Noodle, Stroganoff Style. I have a gas oven, I turn the flames up high. I turn back to Laverne and Shirley and let the words dissolve into laughter. Shirley is injured in a fall, the soup is done, she undergoes a personality change, the beef is large and tender, Laverne is flabbergasted and doesn't understand what's happened, the noodles are long and slide quickly into my mouth, Shirley doesn't know Laverne's name, I slurp the dark liquid from the bottom of the bowl, Shirley hits her head on the door, she's cured, the soup is gone.

Poland is now enclosed by its own army. I have one last package of Nabisco's Premium Saltines. It won't last long.

PART III

My diet begins. I have vowed to eat nothing but fruit, Beverly-Hills style. I could eat a cup of blueberries, two grapefruit, an apple, cling peaches canned in water, and a can of fruit cocktail, and still get less calories than a McDonald's fish sandwich. Besides, it is perfect for tonight's menu of Christmas shows: Rudolph, Bing, and Mac Davis.

Christmas means never having to watch something you haven't seen before. How many "Silent Nights" have I heard? How many versions of "White Christmas"? I sit in the warmth of apartment air, dreaming of hours of nothingness under the bitter sun. Burl Ives announces the sad plight of Rudolph, his melancholy retreat into shame, and I am drawn once again into self-pity. I look at the shirt pulled over the stomach and watch it like a mother watches her unborn child. Then I feed at the picture screen's image, the lines and dots shifting like women in dreams.

I eat three apples and two bananas before realizing I have very little fruit in stock. It's a hard decision but I decide to abandon my diet.

When Rudolph becomes accepted into the clan, I turn to the frig. A Kentucky-fried breast and thigh wait for my tongue, two days old but still ready.

PART IV

Why does my stomach seem so empty, that gnawing at the root of my esophagus lasting and lasting? I give it what it wants. I feed it chuck roast and ravioli, Skippy Chunky Peanut Butter, and German Fudge Cake. I let it rest when it wants, no jogging or aerobicise to jostle it from happiness. But it won't stop. On the night before Christmas, it smells what others have, the large turkeys basted in butter, the candied yams, the salted peas, stuffing. It tastes Thanksgiving's pumpkin pie; it tastes it till the burning comes.

I am ready to be comfortable. All day at work, I dream of this. To lie on the couch with my remote control, pushing till the right image comes: Sleepy Floyd catches an overhead pass from the backcourt, dribbles twice, deeks the defender, and makes a twisting reverse lay-up. It is 3 above in Detroit, with a wind-chill factor of -21. Starsky's face is tense behind the windshield as his car cuts in front of a bus. The Michigan holiday death toll is 17 just before Christmas. Ritchie Cunningham has found a job. It is silent in Poland.

I am hungry. The refrigerator is nearly empty. I search it like a spot lit killer. Nothing, nothing but moldy cottage cheese, eggs, and orange juice. No cheese, no Stouffers, no cold meat. On the other side of the apartment complex shines the colors of Christmas, lit on trees in windows. They probably have food too, full refrigerators lined from the catsup container to the leftovers wrapped in Saran.

During the commercial in the *Joker's Wild*, I make the necessary phone calls: The Town House, Fonte D'Amore, Diggers, Mexican Fiesta, The Bone Yard, The Pear Tree, Big Boy's, Wendy's, White Castle, Kroger's. Nothing is open. The panic starts. I flip from the *Mup-*

pet Show to ABC News to *Hawaii Five-O* to *PM Magazine* to Kotter without stopping. Nothing satisfies. Even the *Wild, Wild World of Animals* teaches me nothing. Baretta doesn't care about humanity's suffering. But three X's later on *Tic Tac Dough*, I have an idea. I can't wait for the commercial. The call is made: 425-6723. Three rings, no answer. Shit!

The ringing stops. A woman's voice: "Seven-Eleven, can I help you?"

No words come to my mouth.

"Hello."

I stammer a meek thank you.

The girl says, "What?"

"I'll see you in a minute."

PART V

The road to 7-Eleven is littered with snow and few cars. Everyone's inside, their trees are shining, their windows neon and rainbow-colored. The tables bristle with plates and forks. I shift into third and keep it there, till the light appears, the red, white, and green.

The first spot is open in front of the door. The girl looks out from her book to see who's arrived. It's me, I want to yell, the man on the telephone. She doesn't look long. Her left foot is perched on the counter. She looks bored.

The bell rings as I enter but she doesn't budge from her book. I can't see the name but there are more important names in the world: Stokely's Chili with Beans, Morton's Beef Patties with Mushroom Gravy, La Choy's Pepper Oriental Chow Mein, Mrs. Paul's Sauerkraut Pierogies, Polish Style. I take them all into my arms and put them on the counter. My tongue is wet. The girl gives my food the eye.

Next aisle: The girl keeps peeking. I hide amongst the soups, the Franco-American Ravioli, with Meatballs and Tomato Sauce. Her eye turns from the book to me. I move to the freezer, latch on to Louis Rich's Roasted Boneless Breast. She has light brown hair that covers her ears and tired eyes, more red than white. I lower my head and search the shelves for coffee and sugar.

It's Christmas Eve and the golden star above the artificial tree turns off and on, a neon God. I am finished. She rings the register, wearing a mint perfume that smells like candy canes. I wait for totals while underneath the counter, a naked woman opens her skirt for me and winks. "$22.49." The girl says nothing else. She has no need for me.

I am ready to buy the woman under the counter and take her home. But the bell has rung, a man walks through the glass door, and it's almost time for *MASH*.

PART VI

I can't satisfy myself. There are no gifts under my rubber plant this morning and there is nothing on TV but sermons and singing. What's the use of waking? There's nothing to do but scramble some more eggs and drink another cup of coffee, to throw away the aluminum trays and put the empty bottles in a bag, ready for transport to the recycling plant. I will probably drink from the same bottle again.

The phone buzzes and my heartbeat speeds. The 7-Eleven girl appears in my eye, apologizes, and kisses my cheek. I give her a chocolate-frosted pop tart, and answer the phone. "Merry Christmas," my mother jokes. I do not appreciate the humor. I am Jewish and not merry.

"What do you want, mom?"

"Are you coming over today?"

"For what?"

"Dinner."

"What are you having?"

"What do you care? You'll eat it anyways."

"I don't think so. I'm just gonna sit home and take it easy."

"I don't care. Don't come." Click.

PART VII

I am so hungry I can't stop eating… so hungry and grateful there is so much in the world to eat… so hungry I've got to eat it before someone else does. Watch the commercials for CARE and you'll realize the world's food supply is limited. Everyday, people drop in the street, stick men unable to find even small amounts of rice.

I am so hungry my stomach cries for Rice-A-Roni, San Francisco Style; it cries for Green Giant Boil-in-Bag White & Wild Rice. I have to eat, I have to empty my plate because other people in the world are starving, they kneel in streets begging others for food, they lie in the street under the flies, who are also hungry and need us too.

But never mind. It is lunchtime, the sermons are over, regular programming has begun again, and Christmas meals wait for tongues and teeth.

But first, a commercial break: A family gathers at a large table, the music is lush, the table shines with plates of white chicken and red cranberries. Smiles and laughter. The wine is displayed, the message is clear: Drink Gallo French Colombard, Eat, and Be Merry.

Old Man Yellow
1978

He sits in the driveway all day,
Looking catatonic, those two rueful eyes
Staring into space. Waiting,

Like a sick dog tied to a foot-long chain,
Waiting my command. "Go already, take off,"
I would say if he weren't born deaf,

If he weren't so senile. He never winks an eye,
But I know his tricks, the games he plays.
You should see him in the rain, snoring,

Groaning. I press the pedal, harder
And harder. He wheezes, then decides to rest.
A sorry sight, my '68 Ford Custom.

Supposedly yellow. His skin turns to rust
(Even the insides are falling apart:
Legs, heart, stomach lining.) No,

I won't sell him or send him to the "Home,"
The junk resort where old men come to die,
Their massive buttocks squeezed

Into square steel molds, or amputated,
The head and arms ripped apart. No,
Old man, you're safe with me. You know

Your home. We belong
To each other, both lazy, stubborn,
Waiting, waiting.

For You (on your 21st birthday)
1978

The spiders are back.
90 degrees and the spiders are back.

You, black point,
scurrying across the ceiling,
didn't I snuff you out last year?
I dreamt of reincarnation,
of waking up like you, scurrying, escaping,
but that didn't stop me.
After every page, you changed your spot,
near the light, above my head,
on the horse's eye of my *Guernica* reprint,
or plunging down your clear white line,
faster, faster. I had to do it.
You gave me no choice, tempting me,
Outmaneuvering me. I'd wake suddenly,
your spindly legs tugging at my eyelid.

Why do you come back, black ghost, King Hamlet?
Here's your revenge, here's my eye, bite it.

The tissue paper is rolled up, ready to go.
Black octopus, you jump from me,
Scamper as fast as you can, breathless,
afraid. For what? What's your life?

Stand still. Forgive me.

The Recoil
1978

I have a recurring dream: waking
In a Skinner box, electric bullets

Shot through my veins. The rest of the night
I spend diving at walls and never reach the bar.

I wake to a surging sun,
Put on sunglasses to hide me from her

And go to school where we crush bacteria
On our slides or sit like bacteria,

400 of us, to a drone from a podium,
Where in front of me is a mound of thick and fluffy hair.

Oh, how I'd love to fling myself
At her, to slash her wax with a knife

But no. The shock comes
And I leap.

A Bad Poem
1978

It wilts faster than the flowers
I gave you. Starts out looking bright,
a myriad of colors, pink, red, and white.
Before you know it,
it's just flashy or trash,
jumbled words
without the right connection,
meaning nothing. Before it's over,
it changes the subject,
tries to rescue itself
from the imponderable conclusion.

I gave you one on your birthday,
hoping to say
what I couldn't tell you.
It never worked. Now,
it's dead
like the flowers;
the pink's turned mauve,
the white black.
I threw the copy in the trash.

Reflections on a New Year Casualty
1979

I
It comes with perilous speed:
headlights swerving on the black road,
white lines like scars of light.

The snow begins in slow syncopation,
you wait for the car-eyes closing in.
The snow thickens. No one comes.

II
On the TV screen, cars erupt
like suns, flames scatter in red clouds.
But there is no pain,

No dark infinity. On the News,
there is just this:
one more certified dead.

III
When I sleep
amidst the night sirens,
the flashing lights like suns

I see into the white cars come
bodies with red faces
and all their darkness covered in white.

pieces
1979

a woman I accidentally touch, her eyes
stabbing mine for one dream-second

my lab partner, inquisitive and dreamy,
the girl at the movies who whispers and giggles,

who thought she knew me. one quits school,
the other walks out in the middle

a quick escape. a continuous leaving.
and now my ex-teacher, poet, friend,

gone to Saskatoon through wind and tunnels
with pieces of me scratched on paper

myself being ripped away
from myself

Blurred Vision
1978

When his grandfather died, Robert was surprisingly calm. He had expected a dull, thick pain to mold inside his stomach and rise through his windpipe like vomit, the kind of ache he'd felt after reading Hardy's *Jude the Obscure*. When his mother lost her smile on the phone, he asked her, "Is it Zadeh?" He knew it was; she could hardly speak. He had expected this all along. Every time his mother would suddenly turn quiet on the phone, her eyelids squinting, the wrinkles rising to her forehead, he thought of a thin man naked on a white bed, unable to raise himself to speak. Zadeh finally succumbed, Robert realized. He stared hard at the gray window of the TV, its light rising toward the white ceiling.

A rerun of *MASH* was on but the mouths moved without sound. It was some kind of strange ballet: bodies, eyes, movement, circular movement. His mother sat on the kitchen chair, unable to move. "Zadeh passed away." Her eyes were covered by a thin glaze of water but it didn't slide down her cheeks. It wasn't her father. Both her parents were already dead. "He was taking a nap and he died. There was no pain. He died in his sleep." She could barely speak and she couldn't look at her son. When he was thirteen and she told him of her mother's death, they both wept, a duet of tears, she on the arm of the chair, he into the pillow of the couch. It was such a shock.

Now, he was prepared.

But he was just at the Home two days ago and Zadeh was perfectly normal, resigned and grouchy. "The food's still terrible," he complained to Robert in front of a nurse. "All I eat's the cottage cheese." His nose was reddish. The rest of his face was pale.

"I brought you some pineapple juice and white wine. How are you?"

"Not too good, meinkin."

"What's wrong now?"

"I can't get enough sleep. I'm always tired. That man next to me plays the TV when I'm trying to sleep. You've heard how loud it is. He's almost deaf. Do you know if they sell some kind of ear plug?"

"Radio ear plugs. I used to have one. 'Member the radio you bought me? It had an ear plug."

"Can you get me one?"

"I'll see, I'll see if they sell 'em separately."

Robert forgot all about ear plugs, forgot all about his grandfather until the phone call. "You don't need ear plugs now, Zadeh," he whispered to himself as he stared at the white spotty ceiling of his bedroom. "To die, to sleep," he whispered, his back pressed hard against the soft gray sheet of the unmade bed. "No more; and by a sleep to say we end the heartache" ...he always wanted to say those lines on stage. He twisted his back to the left, "to die, to sleep." He looked at his empty green-felt chair, a rocker, and wondered how he could sleep now.

He could imagine himself on the pulpit in the funeral home, giving the eulogy. He would be wearing a white shirt without the tie. "Morris Ross," he would begin, came from Russia when he was ten, abandoning his family and the pogroms that followed them. He wandered from city to city as a kid. He married sometime before the war to a woman named Rachel whom I never met, whom I was named after. They finally settled in Detroit where he supported his family as a kosher butcher. They had seven kids, three boys, four daughters as well as a few miscarriages and still births. He made $12 a week in '39. The two eldest boys went to war in '42. The others were living in camps. He wasn't home very often. His wife had her third nervous breakdown in '43. The boys came home alive. Rachel spent the rest of her life in a mental home. She died in '55. The two youngest daughters had just married and moved to California. They're here now. Will you please take a bow, Denise and Judy?

"After all his children married, he retired and lived on Social Security in a small flat in Detroit. He had four coronaries, spent a lot of time in California and Sinai Hospital, where I was born. His kids gave him money. He loved his grandchildren more than his kids. He loved to walk down Seven Mile by himself, until he was eighty and needed a cane."

Robert couldn't think of anything else. He turned on his stomach and stuffed his face in the pillow.

Three weeks earlier, before the big Thanksgiving dinner, he had dreamt of his grandfather. Robert was coming down the hall of the Home to see him. Zadeh was completely blind now, unable to move from his wheelchair. Robert just stood there and watched him die. They covered his face and transported him into a room at the end of the hall. The sign on the door said DO NOT DISTURB!

Maybe it was the paper on *King Lear* he was supposed to write that helped spur the dream. It was so depressing, *King Lear*, that is. And his grandfather was a lot like Lear. They were both stubborn, foul-tempered, and hungry for their family's love.

Zadeh was the first to arrive for dinner. He was downstairs sleeping when Robert came downstairs. His neck was bent forward, his head tilted downwards. Robert sat there with him, waiting for him to wake, his hand on his grandpa's knee. The knee was mostly bone, protected by a little flap of knobby skin and silver-black plaid pants. The football game wasn't blacked out. Washington was at Dallas. Dorsett had just been stopped for a two-yard loss. Zadeh's arm was warm so Robert leaned his right arm against it. Zadeh woke when Billy Dupree dived for a 24 yard touchdown, the Dallas crowd leaping to its feet in unison, an explosion of hands. "I wish Detroit would have gotten him," Robert's father, who was on the green recliner, said, half-talking to Robert.

"You know you never even said hello," his grandfather spoke, realizing who it was sitting next to him. "I didn't think he'd be that good when he was at Michigan State, but look at him now. What a catch," his father continued. "How are you?" his grandfather said. "Uh, so-so." "So-so? What's the matter?" "Ah, nothing really. I just don't like to admit to feeling well." The Dallas cheerleaders were waving their arms in unison, their breasts bopping with the beat. Robert was getting a hard-on. He crossed his legs for a moment, jumped up from the chair and told his grandfather he'd be right back.

He didn't come back, at least not until dinner. He had too much to do and he could only take football in spurts. Besides, the paper on Lear was due Monday and he hadn't started yet. You can't write about Lear in one day, he told himself. But it was no use; he didn't feel like writing, especially with all the noise downstairs. He closed the door, turned on the Who's "Behind Blue Eyes," but he could still hear the relatives opening the door, their feigned bursts of joy. "Oh, you look so wonderful," "Oh, it's so great to see you!" It seemed to him whenever the family would meet, they had to shout their hellos, as if elevating their joy would somehow explain why they hadn't come over in nine or ten months. A good burst of polite, warm deceit could soothe the most intricate suspicion.

Robert came down to present himself and deliver his, "Hi, how are you's?" They were all smiling, trying to shift inside the crowded kitchen. The women hugged, the men plopped themselves down to see the third quarter of the game. The women revealed their jellos, pumpkin pies, yams, salads, potato casseroles, and bowed down to get a peek of the turkey in the oven. God, it's a big one, they clamored. Robert tried to get through to get a drink of water. He kissed his aunts' cheeks, all five of them. How handsome he was, what a nice shirt, how's school, did he decide what he wanted to be yet? He made it to the living room and sat next to his Zadeh, who didn't know the meaning of polite love. Dallas was killing Washington. The crowd was almost laughing. Zadeh asked, "Where did you go? I thought you'd be right back."

"I had to do my homework and clean up my room. It was a real mess."

"A real mess, eh? You're a real mess, aren't you?"

"I'm serious. You should have seen it. Records all over the place, blankets and underwear on the floor."

You can't wait till later to clean it? You can't sit with me for more than ten minutes?"

Robert sat still for twenty minutes, happy to be scolded.

His Zadeh didn't seem interested in the gathering, even though he was the grand ancestor, the head, the progenitor of the entire family. They were mostly his. They evolved from his semen. They shared genes if nothing else. He stared at the TV, trying to make out who wore what jersey. The doctor had told him his right eye was blind; there was 20% vision in the other. But his glasses were still in his coat pocket, the edges sticking out. Robert tried to imagine the blurs, the colors fading into each other. His grandfather said to him as he brought out a letter from his pocket, "Robert, I can hardly see anymore. Will you read me this letter?" Every time they talked, he told him he could hardly see anymore. It was hard to take, for both of them. What could you say to someone going blind? Nod? Say, "I'm sorry?" His grandfather's body was slowly shriveling into a casing and a flimsy one at that.

"Zadeh, the letter's from Anne: 'Dear Zadeh, I'm sorry I haven't written. I know you think I'm a bum but I'm not.'" Zadeh laughed at that. "'I wrote twice before but when I finally got around to sending them, I couldn't find them. How's the weather over there? Did it snow yet? Everyone is fine over here. School's okay, but I hate the bus ride. It makes me sick, literally. I'm trying to collect for United Way but I can't get very much. The fortunate don't seem to care too much for the less fortunate. Well, I have to go now. We might be able to come to Michigan in the spring. I really hope we can. I miss you. Love, Annie.'" Robert turned his head toward his grandfather who was just sort of smiling, quietly, treasuring the letter, his right eye almost shining in the lamplight. Annie was a cousin of Robert's from California. He'd seen her once when she was five. Now, according to his Zadeh, she was fourteen and "big as an ox." "Her birthday's next month, December 17th. Robert, you better remember it. You gonna send her a card?"

"I don't know. I'd like to but you know me."

"Yes, I know you. You didn't send me too many letters when I was in California, did you?"

"I sent you a few."

It was December 14th when he died. He had probably already sent her a card with five dollars in the middle. He always sent five dollars. The card probably said,

This is a special day for you
Things are bright, everything's new
I wish you the best for your days ahead
Filled with love and roses so red
Happy Birthday

Robert sat on his green felt chair, pen in hand. He wanted to write Annie but he didn't know what to say. What could he tell her now? She was a kid who barely knew Robert. "This is your cousin, Robert," he began to write. "Remember me? Happy Birthday. Zadeh sent his love before he died." He crumpled the paper and threw it in the trash.

Downstairs, his father was sitting on a kitchen chair, discussing arrangements on the phone. "Tomorrow, yes, we'd better. You take care of the obituary. Sharon will pick out the coffin. I'll call up the funeral home. Alright, call you later." He rose and slowly entered the living room and sat in his favorite spot, the side of the couch facing the TV. CBS was in the White House. Carter was addressing the newsmen about the Mideast. Robert's father wiped his glasses and put them back on. He crossed his arms, the fists under his biceps, and stared at Carter. Carter always seemed to be on the verge of breaking into laughter, even during the most solemn moments. That's why he couldn't stand him.

Robert wasn't about to interrupt. He sat still, trying to read the paper. His father once told him, "Your Zadeh lived a good long life. You don't have to feel sorry for him." Zadeh was in serious condition in Sinai at the time. They were trying to prepare. It was his fourth heart attack. When they saw him on the bed, his head uplifted above the white sheets, Robert felt absolutely powerless. Zadeh looked so small and skinny. He had dropped below 100 pounds. Before, Robert would give his pants to him and they'd fit. Now, his arms were gaunt. There was a cord attached to his chest. The white cropped hair on his head looked even thinner. Robert hated having to see this. He turned to look outside the second story window toward the parking lot which was very large, spreading all the way out to Six Mile Road. It was slightly foggy out. There was a mist of rain covering the window. His father asked Robert if it was raining out. He said it was. His grandfather asked, a dry-throat whisper, if he could move the radio closer. He wanted to hear the ball game. He once told Robert how he had known Ty Cobb and Mickey Cochrane. He used to cut their meat. He said, "That Cobb was a real bastard."

From the front window, Robert could see almost nothing but white. The snow peaked against the sides of the houses as if attracted magnetically. Two little boys threw themselves into it and flapped their arms, trying to become white butterflies. On this, the day of the funeral, Robert tried to go backwards, remembering the stinging of snow against his reddening face as he flew from the porch of the old house to the deep, deep coldness covering the lawn. He and a friend, a face he could hardly form now, used to see who could jump the farthest, who could bury himself the deepest. Robert, the better athlete, would somersault like a rolling snowball and land almost as far as the front tree. His Zadeh would have advised him to "be careful, be careful."

Most of the time, Robert didn't care about being careful. Once, when he was three, he got into his father's Rambler and locked the door. His nose was even with the bottom of the wheel. He yanked the transmission into neutral and felt himself slowly sliding down the driveway. A sudden stop and he jumped from the seat, startled and scared. The front fender of the car, his father told him later, had been slightly dented. Robert had a strange, lost feeling when his father and grandfather both ran out the front door. Their large, gaping mouths pressed against the car windows. "Open up," they yelled but he kept the doors locked. What he remembered most was the color of his grandfather's face, like an overripe nectarine.

The last time his Zadeh was over at the house, he didn't notice the color of his face. When Robert came in the living room, his grandfather was sleeping; his neck bent forward, the head tilted down. Robert sat there with him, waiting for him to wake, his hand on his knee, which was mostly bone, protected by a little flap of knobby skin and silver-black plaid pants. A Washington-Dallas football game was on. Zadeh's arm was warm so Robert leaned his shoulder up against it. When Billy Dupree dived for a 24 yard touchdown, the Dallas crowd leapt to its feet in unison and his Zadeh opened his eyes, realizing who was sitting next to him. "You know, you never even said hello," he told him, and asked how Robert was. "So-so," he told him, knowing that "what's the matter," "nothing," "you can tell me what's the matter," and then "everything's fine" would follow. His Zadeh told him, "Meinkin, I can hardly see you anymore." Robert knew there was nothing he could do.

The football game was dull and Robert was tired, so he rested his head on his grandfather's knee, laid on his side in the fetal position, and tried to sleep. His Zadeh's thigh was bony and uncomfortable. Robert closed his eyes, feeling the moisture of a palm on his ear, the warmth of breath on his neck.

Two
Ghosts of the Fathers

*1979 Winner of the Wayne State University
Tompkins Award for Undergradute Poetry*

After The Fact
1979

You empty two white cups to the sink,
the coffee spills. Two white cups,
the black oozes to the drain
like darkened blood.
The chicken in the stove turns to rust,
the smoke from your cigarette
a whiter shade of gray.

Through your window, you can hear them:
the faint mumbling of kids screaming
"run, run!" They don't know screaming.
They don't know you,
who sewed the velvet swastika
as the striped shirts filed by,
silent, staring at the thickened dirt.

The timer-bell rings. Smoke rises,
oozing out of the stove.
For a second, the roasted chicken
is someone you know.
For a second, it's just bones with two eyes,
rising in a pile like firewood,
dark-crusted firewood.

"Father,"
you can hardly breathe,
"father,
disappear."
You can hardly breathe,
the smoke still rising,
breath from another world.

Rings
1979

Picture a tree that squirms and sways
in the heavy wind, its leaves falling
like hair, slice by slice. It is July,
the "sultry" month. Our front yard tree is sick.
You tend to it with your spatula and specs,
slipping your hand between branches,
rubbing the bark slowly.

Even trees age, the dull-green leaves
tumbling onto the yellowing grass. You rake,
rake, slapping the grass
in a short chopping motion, downwards.
You stand for a moment and look toward the street,
the sweat running down your cheeks, the street
running through your eyes.
I can hear your breath from here.

The tree is quiet. It doesn't shake at all
as you loosen a slice of rotting bark
and peel it like a brown blister.
You can count them: one ring gone.
Fifteen rings, fifteen years ago,
I saw Grand River from this tree,
straddling a high branch, you shaking
your tiny fist below.

Father, do you hold your pain
beneath the bark
as you chop each branch?
Do you bear your ghosts,
firm and poised,
and bury them into your back
and arms as you call the city
to "cut him down?"

Card-players
1979

I
You see, here they sit, prattling,
passing the hearts and spades,
talking one against the other
without pause, "Reena's getting...
ah, that's crazy... Fernwood?
Pass the nuts."

Francis, babbler ultimata, is getting old,
the paunch growing, her under-eye crescents
deepening. Ornca, my mother tells me,
is going a little nuts. She raved one night
of the old country and needed sedatives.
And my aunt with her incessant smoking—
She has a kind heart which, the doctor says, is shriveling.
Even my mother's on her way. Her hands
can hardly hold the ace. You can almost see it
behind her eyes.

II
So when I read your poem on Auschwitz,
the bones like "stacks of matches,"
I thought of them, the four cronies
every Wednesday around the circular cedar wood table.
I know their pasts:
the sharp slanted fences, the charred skin;
how they turn now—the faces of their fathers,
gaunt and scarred, are lost, irretrievable.
My aunt's nine brothers and sisters "in law"
are buried in another country.

III
Sometimes, I see from the stairs
shadows swaying and rising.
Fenced in, unable to budge the dry-wood door,
the windows tightly clamped,
my ancestors huddle, whispering,
"what will happen?"
There's only one table, so they sit.

In this suburban Montecito, this air-conditioned,
blue-walled sanctuary, we meet at last:
my black-haired grandmother
and her roving-eyed father;
my uncle's two sisters, one pale-cheeked,
with short curving red hair, the other
not older than ten, a bright-eyed chirping magpie.
I can hear it begin again, the rising banter,
indecipherable voices, shadowed hands
passing the hearts,
the king of clubs.

Waking
In the Jewish Home for the Aged
1979

He passes the poster girl lit up, flashing.
In the mirror, his face blurs
The tanned Coppertone legs are gone

Behind him, cars come,
Chasing the wind like generals
In black armor, their huge, glaring eyes

The neon signs look down at him
Like ghosts, floating faces
He once knew—staring

When the sky screams a moment,
His mouth lashed with red glass
The pulse slowed to a screech

He wakes
The street outside a long gray vein
The nurse's face large and white

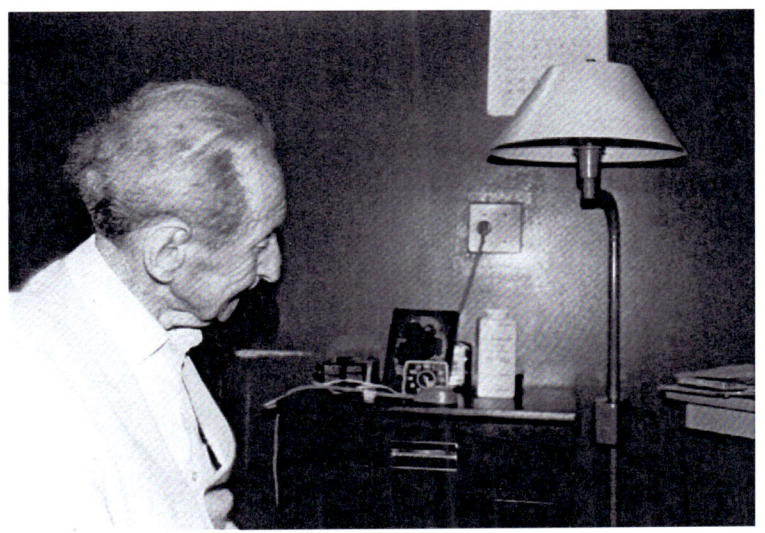

My Zadeh.

On Your Birthday
1979

When the TV turned eleven
and you turned forty-five, we watched it
play all night in all its drunken brashness,
both of us staring, quiet and satiated.

The wind we felt
the furnace breathed. The sun was paroled
from bulbs, carefully shaded
and the wood-grained dull-green box
talked all night:

A man would stick Nebraska
with a wand, turn his coat to snow
while stalked men, shedding oath-of-office smiles,
fled mist to rain. You stared
but your eyes were in stalling cars,
packages of keys, receipts, in snow.

Father, where are you now?
I remember that vibrancy, how I shivered
when your shouts pumped faster
than your heart; or pushing bread
into your mouth, telling me scores
or facts of work.

Now, you sleep,
head slightly twisted on the couch,
arms folded, your eyelids
brown shadows through your wide rims.
And your face, thicker now,
dies into mine,
slightly off-focus,
a lined screen.

Three
Pass Away

Extranjero
1980

And so it's the heart of summer and so
the air seems to be festering
under the great god of dragons. The sun
has the breath of fire, it throws white light
against the crumbling walls. You remember
enough Spanish to know "ciento" stands for heat.

A small man waits outside your hotel,
curly black hair greased and flattened
to cover patches of skull-skin. He holds out
his marionette girl—the few immobile strands of hair,
the limbs flapping epileptically.
You have two prepared replies: "No hablo espagnol,"
"No tengo dinero." He waves his creased hand,
dances the doll under your chin. You can't refuse one
whose hands smell of wax.

Linda tells you this is the city of bargains.
She takes the Spanish girl with the guitar attached to her hand
and dances the wooden shoes on your hair, smiling,
her red lips parted to expose the white.
She thinks it's romantic. She turns her head
away from the black and brown bloodhound
whose ribs bend out of the skin like lattice
under a wet sheet.

You gather her hand in yours, feeling at home
in the sweat of flesh, pointing out familiar faces:
the bunny in the magazine stand, *El Exorcist* on the marquee,
McDonald's. She keeps her silence,
her glimmering eyes turned to the chicken
revolving under a basting brush, the flies gathering.

The Echoes Of The Dead
1979

Walking the hall, you keep looking up
at the long fluorescent light, not wanting
to turn your eyes but doing so. The doors
are like those imaginary ones designed for dreams.
Each number, each hand waves you on
to the end of the hall where your grandfather waits,
his wheelchair still.

Only the woman in #29 groans, legs pinioned
on the sheets, arms waving. "Come here,"
she says to you with her eyes.
She doesn't know you're not the nurse,
the black one who passes on your left, bellowing,
"You want Channel 4, Mrs. Stein?
It's *Bowling for Dollars*, Mrs. Stein."

At the end of the hall, your grandfather
bends into his chair. You touch his back.
He asks you, "have you come to change the sheets?"
When will you change the sheets?"
Even if his legs could rise from the chair,
even if his dried eyes could see,
what could you answer?

In this dream, you wait for
the nurse to turn out the lights,
to cover his face
with her long white sheet. There's nothing
you can tell him now. You try,
but your mouth can barely move
and he can't hear you anyway.

Empty Chairs
1979

In this small dark room
silence sits by itself
on thin legs of wood
brown backs slightly tilted
to the back wall

Through the window
a thin scar of light
lands on one
and disappears
the way it came
behind the yellow curtain
into the shadows

You wish you'd brought your Kodak.
The family in the crevice between crack-stone buildings
is selling bread and staring at you:
"Usted, el extranjero."

"It's good," you tell the old, white-haired woman
with teeth the color of wax. You stammer the words
as you tear off the warm crust with your molars.
"Bueno," you repeat and this time she nods her head.
Linda tugs at your shirt but you're stuck here,
explaining it to yourself: these dark, shadowed faces
lurking in a corner hidden from the sun.
The black-haired kids kneel with bread
on stone. They look up at you like Vietnamese
found in shacks after fire. You can't think
of the Spanish word for "forlorn." All that comes
is "el polvo," the dust.

In the corner of your third-floor room
in the Hogar de Los Angeles, you have felt the dust,
making love under plastic lights—eyes closed,
her mouth contorting like a strange dream,
muttering sounds. You put your hands along her spine
and slid with the sweat. The red lips
parted for your tongue. "Bueno, bueno," you stuttered,
not knowing where the words came from,
not even, that moment, feeling them rise.

Passing
1981

In the wind you can hear the ice cream truck
celebrating the new summer,
a nursery song you don't remember.
You spend the day by windows,
peeking. Cars pass,
children almost out of school flutter
in a dance you can't quite recognize.

These are the dog days, you remember
from a movie, the days spent under the air-conditioner
smiling because everyone loves the sun.
Your son is playing ball with another boy
you don't recognize. He dives in the nearly green grass
and lifts his arm to show the world
his great catch. You know the feeling.

You name each model of car to yourself
as it passes, the new ones too:
Lynx, Starlet, Aries. Your face is sweaty,
you can feel the TV calling. Your wife
enters from the backyard, her hands dark from the soil
she's been digging. She passes
into the bathroom, the sink begins.

You can imagine a stream of water
dripping from her brown eyelids,
you can imagine the eyes in the mirror
asking themselves questions you can't answer.
You turn your eyes across the street.
Mrs. Zandi is polishing her perfect skin
Into darkness. It's time for your midday nap.

Saturday Night, From a Chair on the Porch
1981

The sun also lowers, purple
flecks rising from its skull,
maroon clouds, shaped like wings,
floating out of the red lights
of the Channel 50 tower.
Just one more swig to close my eyes,

the breeze glazing my cheeks
like the silk-dream of your toes
on my thigh. Tonight, everything's quiet,
no cars, no low whispers. Just a radio,
cross-circuited, plays in my head.

Wakoski said in the News
how everything comes down to the man
who left her with a handshake. Yesterday,
when your eyes entered the window—
two dark suns rising out of the darkness—
I could hardly speak. You said I was aloof
in high school. Yesterday,
you said I had perfect teeth.

That booze-song keeps buzzing in my head.
There's no stopping it, no stopping
the darkness that covers the porch,
no stopping the waiting. I'm waiting
for the darkness, waiting for my favorite dream
to take me—the one about us
living out our eternal dream. I'm waiting
for our last handshake.

When I open my eyes, it's still light.
Across the street, two people
are sitting on a porch,
saying nothing.

Last Call
1981

She takes her hand and waves it,
A large bird darkening my wall.
The window is wide open,
The gold plaid curtains tugged shut.
This is the way she wants it
This last night, the rain coming close
The curtains blown pregnant, the breeze
Showering us in this lamp lit glaze.

We lie still, we don't make a noise.
Our eyes follow our shadowed hands
Across each other's breasts
Crisscrossing on the wall. We are waiting
For the gentle tapping on the sill
To soothe us to sleep
The world to disappear
In the last cool breath of night.

The crickets are talking—
How can I sleep, the warmth
Of her neck wetting my palm?
The rain whispers as if it knew
The language of loss, as if it could
Imagine her high heels
Tapping me away from her porch steps
Like Morse signals… g-o-o-d-b-y-e.

What shadows dance under the closed eyelids?
When does her breath—the slow warm breeze
On my arm—become the wind
And float away? In sleep, she lets
Her hands fall on my chest,
Her knees curl inward like a child's.
I take my hands from her thighs
And hold them steady in the light.

Blood-Breath
1982

I
It's dark again, seven porch lights
peering like stars through my window,
like matches. Something's moving in the wind.
Not the sea-shell whisper of traffic,
the wheels like waves licking the concrete.
Not even the garbage can rattling across the street.
This is just a pause, maybe leaves, maybe
Prayers on tongues.

I want to thank someone for warm blankets,
for this letter on my bare lap. It brings back
the flapping of curtains keeping you awake,
the breeze flitting across your face. Now,
everything sounds like sea-lapping, like the rubbing
of cheeks with your husband in Mt. Clemens.

This is for the imaginary child, this is it:
Our last sharing.

II
One dream says Christmas, says children
are supposed to be seen, not heard.
"What does that mean?" you ask your father
on his lap. He holds your brown hair, long even then,
between his fingers and says he's sorry.
Through your window, colored lights flash
and fade. Everything moves: reindeers flying
on the flashing screen, you, gliding on his lap,
swaying in the darkness. The furnace coughs
and you both laugh.

These walls ring with laughter, with memories
of the high school chorus singing, "Noel,"
of the slant-yellow light slow-dancing
under our door. This is your prayer for darkness,
for waking under foreign snow.

III

Let me sleep. Let me wash under snow
the gasping for breath, the closed eyes.
On Christmas, I wrapped this blanket
around your shoulders—you shivered so much
you could hardly breathe. I'm still holding,
listening for leaves, prayers on tongues,
tongues in jars on the high school biology shelf.
This wind has a formaldehyde tongue—the stillness
of small bodies floating, cords still attached.

This is my last prayer: Open its eyes,
let it feel the blood-breath, the bathing
of wind, your hands. Everything covered
by your thin, scared hands, their warm wrapping,
your breath bathing us in our last sleep.

IV

These papers covering my bed tell all:
the death of your father, of your unseen child.
The wind sucking out the dead future
the size of your unwrapped fist. How could
it ever breathe so small? How can the wind
breathe now? So dark, so still.
The cars gone, the leaves asleep.

Snapshots
1982

I
Christmas, we held hands by the tree,
No words but hands, warm, not letting go,
Two hands in a séance of light,
Green bulbs, and the star of Christ
Above our heads. You whispered
In my ear what doesn't remain.
Only my eyes remember:

Two champagne glasses, white stars
Rising in them. A man is drowning there.
His words fly up in bubbles,
White flies burned in the light
Of candles, in my gaze
When your brother snapped the shutter.
I didn't smile or keep the pictures.

Your eyes were white, your mouth sad.
I looked so out of place.

II
Your hair looks almost olive-green
In this photo, a Botticelli swaying,
A wild, windy tousle. Your eyes, green too,
Seem frightened, sun-shocked I think.
How could I forget the warm smell
Of their tears, my finger the swab,
And rubbing your lids shut?

Now, things drizzle backwards,
Slow-motion, cloudier even than your eyes
In memory, or here, out of focus.

The way you stand against my car, not caring
Where your fingers point, beige lines
Stretched against blue metal flesh. The secret
Inner life of fingers, bloodlines, bending

Away from me toward warmth
Even the sun can't provide.

III

How didn't I see the rain
Your eyes held, the sadness that warmed
Your hands? I think of photos not taken:
Your bare feet, pink and cold, against the chair's,
The wet red lines of your eyes leading nowhere,
The last flight of your hands
From my cheeks, my hair, into the rain-drenched night.

I can't see through chill of glass,
Through windows wet with rain, your still body
Asleep, somewhere. The rain won't end
Its splash against windshield. My tires draw lines
Through it, the traffic lights glaze in the puddles.
Sandy, these are my last pictures of you:
Your pained eyes headlights, the wipers your arms

Waving. You're dead,
Wave me away.

Lines
1983

Two stretched fingers equal half a country
But I can feel your breath from here

Sliding across the burnt-orange hills of Tennessee,
Hills sliced by concrete that wanders
Like a cut vein into the lost heart of Michigan—

Auburn lines of wheat under snow, pieces of cars
Coming up the line, rolling highway thunder—

Into my dwarfed hands. The full aroma
Of your voice that can only be felt now
Through the telephone line, transparent,

Gliding into my left ear. In another land,
Sunshine polishes your cheeks,

The wind circles the earth your hands touch.
Here, in the hawk-shadow lit from above,
I feel the snow's glare through my window,

Only imagine the sinking of hands, ours,
Inside that cold whiteness.

At four in the morning, in this lamp-lit room,
It's all wind-moan of furnace
And ticking. Insomnia is a ceaseless ticking

Of nerves, of hands still groping
For warm skin, for the delicate red lines

In your wrist. Did you want to sever them,
That night, in the darkened basement,
Bearing your pain alone, the shaking?

I measure the inches from your eyes
On this map, the points of water dropped

Into your palm, the whispers you cannot hear
Floating through the frost-glazed window
I leave open. It's 28 and falling,

My eyelids fall, bearing the weight
Of loss: sleep, sun, you,

The midnight calls, the lines
On your palm that once pointed to those
I raise to my temples now.

As if words hid there, shadowed
In the fork and cross. As if

To blot out snow meant crossing
This unpaved road, meant landing
Beyond darkness, in the sweat of your arms.

Pass Away
1985

Pass away the clock,
The heart skipping its own beat.
Pass away the heartache
That holds you silent
Like a watch
Without a second hand
A hand without nerves.
You can pass out
From so much drink
That you forget where your
Hands are, or who held them
So many years ago.

Three years before
You could call him
On the phone, you could
Whisper his name
In your sleep
You knew where he was
You knew you could wake him
If you had to.

Pass away the sky
That holds the water and heat
It can shoot a spark
Far into the heart of
Wood and send shivers
Into a young boy's heart.
Two weeks ago,
Two boys felt
The wood collapsing
Over them, the branches

Shaking like bats
In the hands
Of giants. They felt
Their breath move away
Like smoke from flung
Cigarettes.

Last Saturday, the thirteenth,
A young girl watched
Her pain dissolve like nicotine,
Her face, what was left of it,
Her eyes only seeing whiteness
Of the distant room,
Slowly shutting. A girl
Who had cancer two-thirds
Of her life,
Choking in her heart's silence,
Melting in the bitter sweet
Mother's tears,
Six operations not enough,
Nine years too much to hold
The gentleness of a little girl.

Pass away into the midnight
Howl of loss, the sharp
Tear of "he will never be here
Again." Pass away the photo
You hold in the sweat
Of your palms, the weak
Smile of a boy who
Never passed into puberty,
Who never felt the hold of a Mustang's
Wheels or the kiss
Of a young girl's lips.

Pass away, my brother,
Into the sad silence
Of the wind,
Into the earth that cuddled
You three years ago
Sunday. Three years,
A boy frozen at thirteen,
His pictures left standing
In the netherworld
Of my head.

Mother
1986

The voice is gone.
Mother sits in a chair
that's broken, matchstick pieces
crumbled under her feet,
the scarred blisters that once
pressed water against the ground.
There is no ground, just stones
without space, and nothing to hold.

Her caesarian heart
waits for his heat,
the last delivery of blood.
Senseless, the curtains
still flutter, the vegetables
must still be cut. Under the window,
Mother wraps her shadow
in his blue and gold pennant

In the bottom of a toy box
in a soundless room.
And on the ledge,
seeds of plants
dry
and crack
like windows against cars.

Echo
1988

I search the photo
For a voice I can't
Remember, a faint laugh
In an echo of clocks.
His eyes speak the tongue
Of shadows, my eyes talk
A world he cannot see.

I catch myself whispering,
In frame-silence, as if
Whispers could be heard
Six years ago. A flicker of light
Doesn't return, though his hands
Still hold the yad
Of a Bar Mitzvah boy.

Imagine his hands
Wrapped around my back,
His fingers clutching
Mine in a faint grasp. Each
July, I see his small hands
Flung against glass, his face
Bruised like a rotten peach.

The decibel of pain is fainter,
Ebbing like blackened water
In the river of my gut. The ache
Is a whisper you hear
At night, in the loneliness of bed:
Munch's Scream of Silence.
He will not grow up.

Twenty One
1989

It's his birthday today.
Home from MSU,
Two weeks to kill,
He shows up on the doorstep,
Taller than me now, thinner,
He shakes my hand.
I wave him in.
He kisses Judy, picks up Kyle,
Swings him over his shoulder,
And they laugh.
"What you got for Kyle?"
Kyle shamelessly asks.
He pulls a green shirt from his pocket:
"My uncle goes to MSU,
And all I got was this stupid shirt."
Ilana crawls up behind him,
Climbs his leg.
He takes her by the hand,
And helps her step-by-step
Tip-toe from the couch
To the lowest stair.

It's his birthday, December
23rd. He's twenty-one,
And now it's time
To go out and sip beer together.
He can throw the fake ID
Away, and we can sit
Man-to-man, sharing
Laughs, memories, the future.

Big screen football plays above.
We talk of the new Lions, Barry,

The Pistons winning it all,
Mahorn in Philly, State in Hawaii,
The Rose Bowl, the end of the Bo days.
We talk of the last ten years,
The eighties, the Bird-Magic years,
The '84 Tigers and their descent.
How much everything has changed,
Even his dreams of becoming
The new Magic have faded,
But his love of sports still burns.

> Remember the days
> We played soccer in the yard,
> Chased each other in the leaves.
> You kicked and scored
> And raised your hands in victory.
> Remember us riding bikes
> From street to street,
> The radio blasting.
> We played checkers on the porch,
> Ping-pong in the basement.
> Together, we were the Fun Boys.
> Twelve years your elder,
> I was your Peter Pan.
> When you were thirteen,
> I was thirteen
> And growing young.

The football game drones on.
I sit on the couch, watching men
In armor and helmets flinging
Their bodies against turf,
Against each other.
I turn off the sound
And hear only the swish
Of my blood pushing,

Rushing through the veins.
How can the blood flow,
Back and forth,
Through the same veins,
The same arteries, day after day,
Without slowing, never stopping?
How can a child,
Flung against metal and glass,
Be stripped of breath
Within two hours?
I see my brother
In the mirror of my eyes
As he leaves. We hug;
He tells me he will see me soon
After graduation. I tell Kenny
I will miss him
But I know he will do well.
He knows in his heart
He cannot lose.

Only the survivors lose,
Imprisoned
In the lonely ache
Of their dreams.

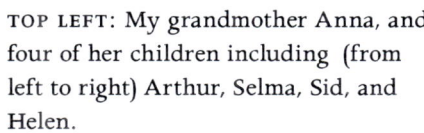

TOP LEFT: My grandmother Anna, and four of her children including (from left to right) Arthur, Selma, Sid, and Helen.

MID-LEFT: My Zadeh and I.

MID-RIGHT: My brother Kenny, sister Leslie, and I.

BOTTOM RIGHT: Me standing in front of my first car, the 1968 Ford Custom.

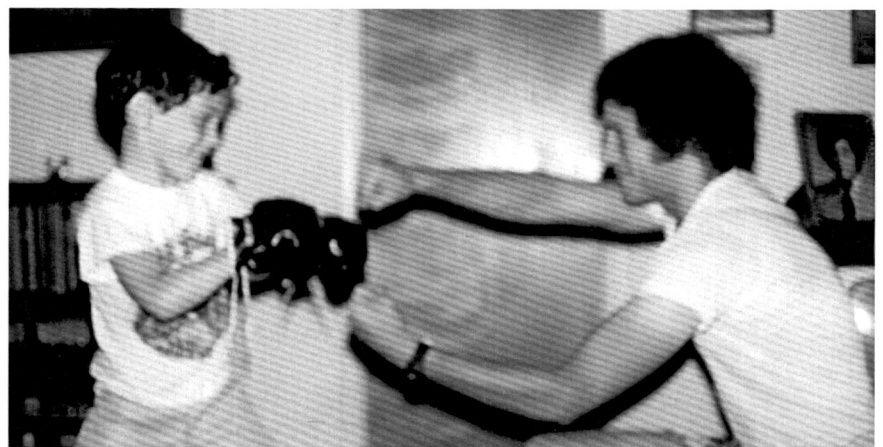

TOP: Kenny and I boxing.

MID-LEFT: My uncle Morey, cousin Mike ("Groomsman") and Kenny.

MID-RIGHT: Uncle Sid ("Remembering My Uncle").

BOTTOM: My father, Milt and mother, Rochelle at their 40th wedding anniversary party.

TOP: My sister, Leslie, brother Kenny, and I at Kenny's Bar Mitzvah, 1982.

MIDDLE: My fiancée, Judy and I on our engagement night, 1984.

BOTTOM: My brother-in-law, Joel ("Down") and son, Kyle.

TOP: My daughter, Ilana ("One Year") and I.

MIDDLE: My daughter Ilana, daughter Marlee, and I.

BOTTOM: My son, Kyle, at a Detroit Red Wings playoff game.

Four
One Year Into Another

One Year
1990

One year ago,
we walked the white halls,
step by step, your mother
and I. Her hand clasped to mine,
afraid to fall, she pushed
past pain, the relentless
squeezing and tearing
that pulled you out
from the soft, wet darkness
to the hospital glare
of strange lights, our faces
foreign. I wrapped you
tight, but you were cold,
those tiny hands, your frightened
eyes, eight and a half pounds
I clasped to my chest,
afraid to let you fall:
that awesome moment
of first love.

One year dissolves
so fast, the end of a decade,
Reagan, the clenched regimes
of Eastern Europe, the beginning
of your life. Out of the humming breath
of sleep, the constant motion
of hands and flailing feet,
blinked a new snapshot,
hour by hour: Your eyes
focused, fingers stretched to my lips,
your lips quivering in a slight smile.
You rolled over and sat up

for the first time, amazed your head
was off the floor. You reached for
the top of the coffee table,
pulled yourself up, and giggled.
I watched you flower
like a filmed rose in fast motion,
the red hues deepening,
the pedals stretching out
like hands.

Today, you shake
your head and laugh
and drop Cheerios in a cup
as if it were a new discovery,
the most ingenious game.
You reach out
to take your first steps,
alone, afraid to drop,
stretching to clasp my outstretched hands.

Ilana, I'm frightened too,
the new decade beginning,
uncertain, perilous, five I know
dead already. Who will you be
in ten, fifteen, twenty years?
What new breakthrough chemical
will cause tomorrow's cancer?
I reach for your little fingers
and squeeze them,
savoring this moment,
your goos and aahs,
your unforgettable
six-tooth smile. Ilana,
I will not let you fall.

Wednesday
1990

Tired, and worn from the week before,
The day begins with dread:
The fear of standing before fifty faces
A fool, with only a gnawing in the gut,
Lost without memory, without words.
Somehow, you know in the end,
Thursday will come.

After work, you recite words to yourself,
Back and forth, repeat, repeat,
And wonder how you'll ever get them
Straight. You drive and time yourself
Against the clock, knowing
They won't laugh at your face,
Fall asleep, or give the News
A scathing review. But knowledge
Will not stop the shaking.

6:30 and you enter the room
With the same people who last week
Made you feel okay. But this is a
New week. Though you now remember
The meaning of support,
The fear of failure clings
Like old worn out socks
You can't throw out.

The wait begins,
The blood stirs. Once again,
You see that everyone gives a piece
Of themselves. Your friends, your teachers
Recite visions etched in their heads,
Moments of hilarity, humiliation,

Wonder, loss, a sense of the shared
Passage of life. Somehow,
You feel a little richer
In spirit.

Your moment arrives
And you push against the pressure
Of your own critic's brain
And give a minute of yourself.
You empty your fear,
Your loneliness into the laps
Of friends who don't scorn or laugh
Or make you feel alone. Instead,
You feel unable to fall,
Held in the shadow of friends.

Sitting down, relieved it's over,
You sense the day Carnegie will be over.
Friends will disappear, scattering
Into their own worlds. You wonder
How it would feel to be embraced by friends
Everyday. But Thursday comes
And you're back again, alone,
In the "real world."

You scrap and curse
And wonder
Where your spirit went.
But a moment comes,
Suddenly. You remember
A phrase someone said
Last night. At once,
Thankful,
You feel renewed,
At peace.

Kenny's Song
1990

The street hums
With the swish of cars.
My son's face turns colors
In bed, the whispered breath
Serene as smoke
Puffed from a winter's tailpipe.
His mouth moves slightly,
His head rolls to the left. I walk,
Searching for clues,
The washed-out pictures repeating,
Flickering in my head.
I search the silence
For my brother's voice: rewind,
Flashback, but no tapes are left,
None but the blurred,
Scratchy tape of memory.

I move my mind to the land
Of missed classes, of games
Without fear. I see his hands
Rising, palms cupping the orange ball.
The ball sails through the net,
A beautiful wheezing,
The swish of lost time.
I touch Kenny's hands
And steer them toward the checkerboard,
The black circles staring upward.
He wants so badly to win, to say
King me, king me.
But his voice is muffled,
An old recording, 78 RPM.

Outside, white-feathered speckles
Parachute downwards, silent,
Clinging to the window.
We move from the register, our bare feet
Brushing against the hot metal,
To the large cold mattress
Of the backyard. We lie down,
Flapping our hands faster and faster.
The sky bright blue, our breath
Like smoke, we become angels
Of snow, rising upward
Toward the bitterness of sun.

The window fills
With frost, Kyle's room empty
Of words. The clock hands
Of Mickey Mouse move so slowly
I can hardly feel their movement.
Every minute's a gift, every memory
A still shot in the gray light
Of night, a dream song
I cling to. I want to stop
Counting the aches.
I want to stop seeing the windshield,
Shattered, Kenny's thirteen-year face
A gray shard, painted
The last time I see him
In plastered makeup.
I want to hold his body,
Whole again, against my chest.
I want to hear his voice.

The street sings
The whirr of sirens. My son
Stirs in bed, shaken,

His three-year old whimper
A dream song I can't comprehend.
From the arms up, I lift him
And hold his ears to my mouth.
"It'll be okay," I whisper, as if I knew
It would, as if I could wrap
My hands around his back
And clench his life
To my chest and hold it there,
On infinite pause.

In the soundtrack of Kyle's heartbeat,
I hear the gentle tap
Of a drum and the whisper
Of a song, suddenly louder,
The beat now brazen.
Kenny's tapping his hands
To his knees and mouthing
The words, "When I was young,
A miracle, oh, it was beautiful,
Magical." He jumps on Kyle's bed,
His arm a sleek guitar, his breath
The color of smoke.
It's his favorite song, "The Logical Song."
"When all the world's asleep,
The questions run so deep," his lips
Quiver, as if he were giving
His last performance.
The drumbeat is fading, the voice
Isn't his, but in the still life
Of the night, the burning
Afterglow of this freeze-frame,
It will do.
It will have to do.

Severance
1996

We called him to Livonia for a meeting.
He didn't ask why he should come three
Hours away, from Crown Point, Indiana.
I prepared a note for his file, the right words,
An apologetic tone, the search
For his understanding. Everything was prepared,
The bonus, the references, the severance pay.

He came on Friday, made his greetings,
Brought back samples. He joked with the receptionist,
My heart racing. I called him into my office,
Sat him down. "I have no choice." Your territory
Is cut and with it your job. You knew
Something was coming, it wasn't working out,
I didn't want to do it, it isn't personal, it's just
Business, I know you'll land on your feet,
There are some good opportunities, I'll write
A nice recommendation.

He tells me he'll have to withdraw
An offer on a house he and his wife just chose.
Bad timing, he says, but it was a stretch,
Maybe a "blessing in disguise." He sits back
In the chair, staring at the darkened woods outside,
His eyes away from me. We talk for hours.
I invite him to lunch before sending him
Back to his Indiana home.

Before leaving, he asks, how was he doing, really?
Is there hope for him? I tell him, "Sure,"
Though not really sure he'll make it. He gives me
Two orders from his briefcase, explains the details,

Asks what should he tell his customers, what will
We tell the employees? I'll work on it, say something
Face-saving, I say. I'll see you soon. I have to get
To my paperwork.

The orders he wrote sit on my desk, waiting for
Monday. The stack of bills awaiting signature
I can't sign. I sit still, staring at piles, the clock,
Trying to get my mind and desk organized.
What's important? What is urgent? What should
I delegate? I want to go home, hold my kids,
Stare at the shows they watch all day,
Take a nap. When you're dying, no one thinks,
Why didn't I spend more time at the office?
The comfort usually drawn from this
Is little comfort. I stare at the woods
Outside my window
Until I force myself
To be at peace.

Breath
1997

we are learning again
how to breath
slowly
through the nostrils
the belly

rising and falling
imperceptibly

we live our lives
quickly
forgetting the air
forgetting what got us

here
in the first place

in the airport
shoes moving forward
backwards always

going
there is no time
for us to see that

there is no time
we are caught
in the monotony
of clocks

the fast movement
of our mouths
and worries
someone else
around us

dead
Tsongas is gone
the cancer in his bone

flashing through
his body
he's gone

Cosby's son
we laughed about
twenty years before
shot dead
on an LA side street

my oldest
daughter turns eight
Monday
when she was one
I wrote about her

trying to take
her first steps
and falling
and falling again
and again

Monday
she is eight and I
will bring donuts
to her class

there is no time
to breathe
so we stop

and we breathe
this day
in Lenox, Mass.
we forget our ages
and bodies

the endless losses
we simply lie back
tense our bodies harder

then harder
then the letting
go nothing
nothing
but breath

To The Goldmans
1997

Letter written to Fred and Kim Goldman
MARCH 10, 1997

I have always felt connected to you. Ever since the news of June 13, 1994 propelled the nation into the tragedies of OJ and Nicole Simpson, the Browns, and your family, the Goldmans, I have felt a strange and sad bond, especially to you, Fred, and to Kim. I have been reading your book, *His Name is Ron*, which hauntingly brings back the horror, not only the horror that enveloped you for the last two and a half years, but the sadness I felt in viewing this tragedy. It also brought back the emotions that my family and I went through fifteen years ago. In some ways, our circumstances seem almost linked.

My name is Arnie Goldman. My brother's name is Ken, but we call him Kenny. Kenny is the youngest child in our family, twelve years younger than me, and nine years younger than my sister, Leslie. Kenny was born on December 23, 1968 on an ice-covered night in Detroit, Michigan. It took three hours for my mother, Rochelle, and my father, Milt, to slide to the hospital, but Kenny was finally born, in the middle of the night.

He was the joy of our family, a wonderful child who became funny and friendly and sports-loving and intelligent and affectionate. He became the life spark of not only our immediate family, but of all our uncles, aunts, cousins, and friends. He was not only the baby of all of our families. He was a unique and special kid... until July 20th, 1982, the night that he and my father went to a Detroit Tigers baseball game in Detroit. On their way home, less than a mile from their home, another car sped through a red light and slammed into my dad's car, on the passenger side.

I lived in an apartment about thirty minutes away and was called to the hospital with no explanations. Your book brought back the terror of the mysterious phone call and my speeding to the hospital, not knowing anything but fearing the worst. As it turned out, my father and brother were both in critical conditions, and I feared that my father would not make it. I never ever thought about Kenny. But right after midnight, the doctors told all the family and friends gathered at the hospital that Kenny had died. The doctors said that he would have been a vegetable had he survived. He had been thrown against the windshield. The force of the colliding car had crushed his skull. He was thirteen.

Your book eloquently brings back the suddenness, the horror, and pain of losing someone so close to you, one minute a wondrous, exuberant boy, the next a lifeless corpse, the joy gone from the body. I remember from this nightmare that I had to tell my father that Kenny had died. I dreaded it, because I knew my father had no idea what happened to Kenny. My dad had been unconscious and bandaged and not talked to anyone. I remember his howl of anguish, that deepest of sorrow-filled regrets, when I told him that Kenny had died. He cried, "it should have been me, it should have been me!"

My father survived and the next days were as fleeting as a bad dream: my mother and I together the first night, desperately trying to survive it and force ourselves to sleep, then the call to my sister to come home from Europe where she had won a scholarship, the choosing of the casket, my father in a wheelchair at the funeral, our last viewing of Kenny's body, so unnatural and mannequin-like, all the scars and bruises patched up so we could bear it. I read your book and the memories became vivid again, both your tragedy and ours.

If Kenny survived, he would have been Ron's age. On June 13, 1994, he would have been 25. Kenny had died seven months after his Bar Mitzvah. As in your book, the memory of Lauren's Bat Mitzvah, with Ron and the family singing and dancing, was like our last great memory of us all together, at Kenny's Bar Mitzvah. We still watch the video periodically, and try to remember the joy and togetherness we all felt, as we shared his entry into manhood, his haftorah, the lighting of the candle with our Zadeh, all the friends and family reveling in life. How could we have know then that we had less than seven months to share it with him?

The person who caused the accident was no celebrity. Her name was Rochelle Meckler, a law student with a lawyer-father. The legal matters were quick, a settlement between lawyers, without bloodstains. We never saw her or her father. We never knew if she had taken drugs or was drunk or was sorry or unshaken. The lawyers kept us apart. My mother raged at the injustice, her son taken away, our brother ripped from us, with just a settlement of money from an insurance company. All we really wanted was a show of grief, of regret, an apology. All my parents received was money. And we learned this: Money Means Nothing. As you know, there is no price for life, not $100,000 or $8,000,000 or $25,000,000. There is no price for life.

I want to thank you for what you've done, your eloquence, your speaking out, the heartfelt love of a father, mother, and sibling. As I was reading the book, I could once again feel close to what you went through. It brought back the crazy, nightmarish months that we all vicariously went through with you as the TV and tabloid-nation story unfolded. I, like so many others, was obsessed with the drama of the events and trials, because it was so horrifying and sad. As the events unfolded and I watched the testimonies, heard the soundbites and read the transcript, it became painfully obvious to sense what happened and who had done it. Some of the only sane moments of the media spectacle were the words of your family, the heartbreaking declarations after watching and hearing about your son's death, the vehemence of your pain and anger.

I, like you and so many others, was shocked by the first jury's verdict and relieved by the second. It was comforting to know that justice can sometimes defeat the tricks and lies of lawyers, money, and fame. But it is still a bitter pill to see a murderer free, at home, with his kids, still idolized by so many. It is hard to know that the person who probably killed your son, your brother, goes on with his life, growing up, enjoying the day-to-day, while our loved ones are simply memories for us.

The pain does subside over the years although it will never go away completely. You will never forget or want to forget who Ron was. You must try to remember the moments of his life and what he brought to you. It is great to see you going forward, trying to do something honorable for others, for Ron's memory and for your own sake. After Kenny's death, it took time to try to get our lives back in order, to go forward. In 1984, I met my future wife, Judy, and we had our first child in 1986, Kyle, named after Kenny. We since have had two more children, Ilana and Marlee. My sister married Bruce, who she was dating in 1982 and who helped her through the tragedy. Just last year, they had their first child, Karenna, also named after Kenny. My mother became a piano teacher, and my father, who was the President of a wholesale distributor that I also worked for, retired in 1994 and I took over as President. My family started a basketball league at the Detroit Jewish Community Center in honor of Kenny, who had loved basketball. It is called the Kenny Goldman Memorial League, and it is still going today, teaching kids aged 6-13 about basketball.

It is still painful, knowing that Kenny never graduated, drove a car, turned 21, voted, dated, married, or had a child. We often wonder what he would have done with his life. This sad wonder never goes away. But you can't go back. All you can hope for is that something good comes from the loss. Our children, I feel, are Kenny's blessings.

I pray for good in your lives. Hopefully, you will be blessed with friends and more family, hopefully children and grandchildren. I hope that you continue to help others deal with their losses and continue to make a difference in this world. And I hope that all of you, Fred, Patti, Kim, Lauren, and Michael, find some joy and peace in your lives.

Sincerely yours,

Arnie Goldman

Forgetting My Uncle
1997

This year has been
one long journey
of forgetting
almost a year
since my father said
Sid was gone before
the first day of our
annual trade show
the classes give-aways
taking orders and giving out
grand prizes to the final winners

Sid had never missed
a show even when retired
he came he schmoozed
he sold what was needed
to sell the day
after he died
one long class
merged into another
and then another

I'd already forgotten
the drawn out months
in a hospital bed with a tube
through his mouth his stomach
his wrist the feeding that
never stopped his mind
dissolving his eyes
slowly shifting from all
he knew into the
netherworld that we

don't know he had
always been around
at home at work
he was there and you
always knew it
he was there

This year has been
one long journey
of forgetting
every day
after work chanting
the mourner's kaddish
in shul before work
until I took the trip
to Phoenix the hot air
soothing my sadness
the sun filling my eyes
and then the trek back
to work the daily routine
waking eating glancing
through the *Free Press*
driving the same route
daily the wandering
of the mind to the
nowhere of the
immediate day

When did his words
the memories lose their
power to cloud
my eyes? When did
his photo suddenly
seem comforting?
Sid's voice now lost

in the sweat of work
the kids' daily tug
of wars

The forgetting
lets us live
but at what price?
My uncle a second
father a trusted friend
lost in the daily drizzle
the mind's puzzle
his grave moved
from one cemetery
to another and even
still I can't go back
to find him

Championships
JULY 21, 1997

The bright sun warms the family room window. The nine dead elms are still against the wind. My parents are standing at their son's gravestone, holding prayers in their hands, a light breeze blowing the pages apart.

I think of Konstantinov lying dormant in a Beaumont bed, eyes closed, enclosed in the mysteries of his mind. His condition: serious but stable. Last night, I watched the new video, *Hockeytown*, a video depicting the Red Wings ascending after forty-two years to their single goal, winning the Stanley Cup. I replayed the electricity of the playoffs, the memory of Yzerman proudly lifting the Cup for the throngs lining the streets in the victory parade, which my son, Kyle, and I had watched from a bus stand on Woodward. For that day, we were absolutely happy.

Two years before I was born, my father, newly married, proudly watched the Wings win the Cup again, for the fourth time in six years. The Detroit sports teams were giants, he recalls, the Lions and Wings yearly winners. He often tells me that I should have seen those teams: Howe in his heyday, Layne the invincible leader at quarterback. "That was a time to be alive," my dad has said, especially the best sports year of all, 1955. Afterward, his mother, Anna, died, the grandmother I never knew, whom I was named after.

In the seventies, Detroit sports were at a low point. The Lions' greatest moment was a playoff game against Dallas. We lost 5-0. The Tigers came close in the Martin years, were exciting with Fidrych, but in the late eighties were often mired in long losing streaks. The Pistons made the playoffs once or twice but ended the seventies with Dick Vitale coaching a dreadful team. The Wings never came close, being the worst team in hockey for much of the decade.

My brother, Kenny, born in 1968, two months after the Tigers' thrilling seven-game World Series win, became the ultimate sports fan. Not long after he learned to talk, he learned sports. He knew all the Detroit and Michigan college teams. He knew most of the players in the "big leagues," memorizing stats, collecting and trading cards. He watched the teams on Channels 50 and 4, even in the worst years. In 1979, finally, he was rewarded by Magic Johnson and Michigan State University with an NCAA Final Four Championship. MSU beat Larry Bird and Indiana State University in a battle of college titans. This was the high point of Kenny's sports life.

In the early eighties, Isiah Thomas brought some hope to the Pistons and Trammell, Whitaker, Parrish, and Gibson brought some spark to the Tigers. The Tigers started showing some promise, becoming a fairly competitive team and climbing the standings. On July 20, 1982, my father took Kenny to a Tigers' night game. On the way home, a half mile from their house, a young law student ran a blinking red light and slammed into the passenger's side door. Kenny was thrown into the windshield glass. He died after midnight. He was thirteen.

The Tigers won that night and in two years won the ultimate prize, the World Series. The city went wild. My fiancée, Judy, and I sat on Alan Trammell's Livonia lawn with twenty others, decorating his trees with toilet paper. Five years later, we celebrated with Isiah, Laimbeer, Rodman, Dumars, and the Pistons, watching every game, thrilled when we beat Magic's Lakers four games to none. My son, Kyle, named after Kenny, was only three, not yet a sports fan. He slept as the Pistons' champagne poured.

After this year's Stanley Cup win, Detroit was alive again with the giddiness of victory. Yzerman, who joined the Wings as a rookie in 1983, had finally gotten his crown. The Russian Five, who had defected from the Communist Soviet Union in the eighties and nineties, had gotten their American prize. Scotty Bowman got his sixth Stanley Cup, on his third team. Finally, after 42 years, Detroit was ecstatic and proud and happy. For five days.

Coming home from a Red Wings golf outing, two of the Russian Five, Fetisov and Konstantinov, along with their Russian-born masseuse, slammed into a tree on Woodward. Their limousine driver had fallen asleep, drunk. Fetisov was injured but within a few days mostly recovered. The masseuse's condition was critical but he has since regained consciousness. Konstantinov is still in serious condition, still in a coma, 29 years old, with a glorious past and unknown future.

Today is the fifteenth anniversary of Kenny's death. He has been dead two more years than he was alive. Whoever remembers him now remembers him for his vibrancy and his humor. He was never happier than when he was watching a game, watching Howe, well past his prime, flicking the puck in off the right goal post or seeing Ben Oglivie hit a low liner over the short right field fence.

Championships are memorable for the memories they create. The championships I've seen and the championships that I may see in the unknown future will always be incomplete. They will be missing a brother to share them with.

From the Jewish Community Center of Detroit's web site, "Kenny Goldman Leagues Heat Up on the Court!"

Summer's Bookends
1997

I
The sun stirs the brown blinds,
Peeking through the window, reflecting
The paper on this desk. All is not lost
In my mind. I sit, my feet
Pulling against each other, trying to
Remember what's lost. The glory
Of this day, its fully sprouted trees,
The begonias beginning to bloom.
All is not lost in memory,
The fathers who've withered and died
In the last month. We go on,
Memorizing the names of the dead,
Not wanting to think of what can
Dampen the light blue skies, the
Soft breeze of a wonderfully warm
May day. Flags are supposed to be
Half-mast. Parades are supposed to
Honor the dead. Today,
We eat the dark brown
Skin of hot dogs, the hamburgers
Char-grilled, ketchup and pickles
Oozing out of the buns.
This is a day when memories
Can't cloud the sun, the toasts
Of glasses, filled with Bud and Coke.
This is Memorial Day,
A day off work,
A day off memory
Of the forgotten dead.

II
The last day of summer
Or so it feels: Labor Day, a
Celebration of work
When we don't work, the last barbecues,
The kids beginning the daily treks
To school. We celebrate labor
In America, like the UPS strike,
Where business has stopped,
The packages resting in storage,
Waiting for delivery. We celebrate
Football and Jerry Lewis,
His MDA charity
Now totaling over 50 million.

Last night, Princess Diana of Wales
Died in a car crash,
Chased by photographers in a Paris tunnel,
Her drunk chauffeur weaving at 120 mph.
I read the news today, oh boy,
Of a princess watched every second,
Every day, her photos rerun everywhere,
The endless stories of her charm, her
Celebrity, her charities. The press
Questions their own obsessions,
The gossip reporters gather
In the darkness of the dead.

Yesterday, I took my son to a Lion's game.
Trying to park, frustrated by $15
Parking lots, we found a spot a mile away.
Walking in the dreary drizzle
Of Pontiac, the dirt-filled lots,
The smoked hot dogs in the tailgates,
The already empty beer cans. Remembering

Fifteen years ago, Super Bowl '82,
San Francisco vs. Cincinnati, Kenny and I
On a three hour car ride in the
Blowing snow, 15 below zero wind chill:
The game almost starting, still
In the car, tired of traffic and cold.
I sold our tickets
Given by Master Lock
for $100 each. We thought
We were rich.
Coming home to watch the rest
Of the game, wondering,
Wondering why. Why did money
Feel empty then? What were we going
To buy with $100? Kenny watched the game
In his room, I listened to rock radio
In mine. Months later in July,
I was called by police to come fast
To Botsford Hospital. At midnight,
His life was over.

III
Labor Day and Memorial Day
Feel reversed. Memorial Day,
Sun-drenched, filled with hope
Of a new summer, a new
Beginning. Labor Day is Diana
Flown back in a box
To Prince Charles, ready
For burial. For comfort's sake,
I turn on Jerry and watch him
Sing his song, "You'll never
Walk alone." It's the same old
Show again, the same jokes,
The tear-filled songs,

The tote board hitting 50 million.
Already I feel guilty.
I didn't give enough.

They're selling Diana's
Dead body shots for $300,000.
And the telethon won't stop
MS from killing kids
The way it has for fifty years.
We throw it more money,
More money, desperate
For a cure, searching
For what? Endings, closure?
Our final mortality,
The answers
Hidden in a box.

Five
Anniversaries

Journal Pieces
1992 – 2002

MARCH 27, 1992

Renewed Marriage Vow to Judy, 1992 – Infinity

I promise to love you and hold you, to give you everything that I hold most dear to me. I promise to comfort you when you're in pain and to share with you my most intimate thoughts and feelings. I promise to be truthful with you, to have the strongest integrity. I promise to be faithful and to always love you, in sickness and in health. I promise to always try to help you be whatever you'd most like to be, to let you be true to yourself. I promise to strive for your happiness and mine, to be a good patient, loving father for your children. I promise to treasure you always, because you are my jewel, my diamond. And you will always be.

MARCH 29, 1992

Today began productively. I went to work early to try to clear away the cobwebs of a missing day, Friday, a day that may have begun a new marriage for Judy and me. I was overwhelmed, walking by a flurry of scattered papers, waiting phone calls, price changes, catalog pages, special orders, past due assignments, a stack of mail, and I began to concentrate and reorganize assignments. I laid out my day for tomorrow and began to read the PRD plans I made in the Carnegie Management class. I was embarrassed to realize I had done almost nothing on my list. Tomorrow, I'll set new deadlines, plug them into the day timer and begin again.

MAY 29, 1993

I'm a little behind with the (Tony) Robbins' exercises but I'm caught up on the tapes. I feel more in control. I've also been reading *The C Zone* and it seems to tie together: Confidence, Control, and Commitment are lessons of both. Throw in fun and pleasure. I'm getting there. States of mind are important to control. Yesterday, in Tape 5, it showed me how to get control of my state the way Cooper did, with a smile, shoulders back, posture straight, breathing deep, and a passionate joyful look. It helped me yesterday, Friday, turning a usually tired, worn-out, stressful day into a fast-paced work day that was effective and good.

Tuesday, I was tired, too slow, uninspired. Wednesday, I had the day off, enjoyed the time with the kids and then went to the game with Kyle and Sid. The weather was gorgeous, 75, and sunny. We saw Harry there, I read the paper, Kyle loved it, it was relaxing. A fun, lazy, enjoyable day...

I hate the medical profession, their high-priced tests, their "specialists," the run-arounds you get, and the drugs and surgery they depend on. It's funny how my yogic, alternative, vegetarian past has interceded in my present now. And I'm glad it has.

Yoga's philosophy, like that of many Eastern religions, says that this life is a preparation for future lives, that the lessons we learn are for the next life. Friday, Judy's psychologist, Dr. Tisdale, was on Kelly & Co. with Brian Weiss talking about past life regression, with people who had experiences communicating with their dead relatives. Tisdale, as well as the book *Who Killed My Daughter?* have changed my outlook to life after death from skeptical disbelief to uncertain acceptance.

JUNE 6, 1993

...one of my goals is to contribute 5% of my income and Hardware Sales' incomes next year. I happened to get lit and info on the lunch at the (Troy) Marriott, which was held by the Cooley's Anemia Association. Cooley's Anemia is a rare children's disease that is fatal. It felt like destiny to be there. Earlier, I looked up phone numbers of good charities. I'll call Monday. I'd called Make a Wish already to get info on how to be a corporate donor.

...another goal is to write a book this year and get it published, whether a small poetry book or an essay or journal book. I'd like to stick to poetry now, because it means so much to me. But to write poetry, I almost need to feel bad. But I feel so good now. At least, I can write daily, whatever it is.

AUGUST 15, 1993

I am at the AMA Course for Presidents and I am feeling fantastic. I've spent one of the most invigorating and relaxing days of my life at the Broadmoor in Colorado Springs. I've exercised, swam twice, walked up to the Seven Falls Canyon, had a phenomenal brunch, laid out in the sun, read from three books, listened to an Alphanetics (speed reading) tape on relaxation. I finished *Principle Centered Leadership* (Stephen Covey,) started notes on a company and personal mission statement... The walk into the Seven Falls was breathtaking and memorable, filled with sun-drenched, awesome views of mountains, clouds, rock formations, streams, and trees. I took some wide-angle photos to capture the views, but nothing can capture the awe-inspiring, god-filled panorama. To walk it made all the difference. I won't forget it.

I found some cards for Judy. I'm looking for a present for our eighth anniversary, but I know what I want to do on our 10th. I want to take her here.

MARCH 21, 1994

It's been a long time since I wrote last. Today, I have to go to Kyle's Seder. I'm searching for balance. That is balance. I need to begin again to write, slowly, carefully, day by day. I have to come out of my shell. I'm reading Covey's *First Things First* and a journal is one of my "first things."

MARCH 3, 1998

It's Rob's birthday. He's supposed to go out with Jeff and me but he was at the Piston's game last night (they won) and tonight, he'll be with his family. I'm two months and 41 years old. Yom Kippur will be on the last day of the fiscal year this year, Sept. 30. I tried meditating today instead of napping, as I've done every morning when I get up. I feel better, but scattered... Sid's 2 year anniversary of his death is Sunday, our show. Sergei Federov signed for 38 million, took the team to Morton's Steakhouse. Czech Republic with Hasek at goal took the gold medal. Lipinsky took gold. Marlee turned 3, Judy 39, Ilana 9. Princess Di has been dead ½ year, Dr. Spock is dying, Henny Youngman dead, Harry Carey gone. We get older. My father and I are going to (attorney) Joel Kellman's tomorrow. Arthur's in the hospital, Judy's parents are due to arrive from Florida today. I'm listening to *The Awakened Life* by Wayne Dyer. There was an article about Metabolife today. I have to prepare for the show, wake the kids. Endless lists, endless lists.

MARCH 19, 1998

Aunt Elsie died this week and I went to the funeral and Shiva at the Doubletree Hotel. A sad affair, not many people, sadness from the immediate family but not from others. She was devoted to her family, the "Yiddishe mom" but overbearing with a mouth that didn't stop, often putting her foot in it. But watching our aunts and uncles disappear is sad, most in their 70's and 80's. Time keeps going, the crush of time, in a faster and faster pace. This day is important, a day to slow down and unwind and remember what's important.

JANUARY 31, 2000

Less than two months ago, Kyle had his Bar Mitzvah, chanting three aliyas from the Torah, the opening service, and the Haftorah. He did beautifully, and I also read from the Torah, with no mistakes. I gave a speech at the Excalibur, and though the food and music was so-so, the Bar Mitzvah with all its planning came and went smoothly.

Everything comes and goes. I am 43 now, ready for our 25th Class Reunion. Norman Allen and Milton Schiffman from Adat Shalom died. I passed my stress test.

How can I slow the time down? By writing about it.

SEPTEMBER 7, 2002

New Year—Rosh Hashanah

It's a New Year and I just began Oasis Inthinity this morning. I need a new start. I am at my highest weight, 225 lbs. I am tired. I look lousy. I feel like crap. I sweat when I sleep. I sweat when I go up the stairs, and I pant. My abdomen is huge. I am sick of being out of control. I ate last night without control. I ate roast beef, chicken wings, kugel, pickles, challah, rice and broccoli, asparagus, kishka, fruit, and chocolate babka. Too much food. It was delicious but once again, I ate too much. I have started with Metafuel this morning. I just took MetaPower and I will take Metaburn later. But the key is eating the balanced high-protein, lower carb, zone-type diet, starting today, and continuing it when I'm at the Weston Golf Outing and at Philly. I'm mildly optimistic. Today is the start of a New Year. Let's roll.

DECEMBER 24, 2002

One day after Kenny's thirty-fourth birthday
Christmas Eve day
A half day at work
Getting up early and exercising
Treadmill, trampoline, power rider, tri flex, yoga
Watching news, taking a shower, shave, Arbonne
Body lotion, drinking Penta Water, Michael Jordan Cologne
Reading *The Power of Now*, Dr. Bob Arnot's
Revolutionary Weight Control Program
While on treadmill, taking 15-20 vitamins
& Metropolol for high blood pressure—channel 932 on
Eating soy nuts, Cereal of Oat Bran
Cheerios, Barbara's Shredded Spoonfuls
With skim milk, green tea with Splenda

Sweetener—focused on the now
And future, a loss of 50 pounds by 12/31/2003
A pound a week, no Lipitor or other drugs
A feeling of health, contentment, control, calm,
Clarity, and confidence
Feed Esther. Give her water and let her outside
Take a deep breath. Breathe the cool air
Coming from the outside thru the open Sunshine
Window. We got a new Pella Patio Door last
Week, beauty, ease of opening, warmth
Thru insulation, seeing the deck lights
Call to me. It's great to be alive.
Seize the Day. Listen to the beauty of soundscapes.
Love what I have
There is nothing else
Right now
Breathe and Be

DECEMBER 25, 2002

    It's Christmas, it's white
    A blanket of snow has fallen
    The snow is deep, the air not too cold,
    The wind a fluffy mix, it feels good
    Esther's been out five times already
    Snuggling her fur into the wet damp snow
    And shaking it off inside the house
    It's a slow day today. Marlee is gone,
    Sleeping at Melanie's...

Ilana is doing the treadmill now; I am staring at a flower stand picture frame with a picture of another family in it. The original purchase from the box. I'll see if I can find a replacement with my family. I have been haunted by an article by Mitch Album about the high school football player killed in a car accident before the State Semifinal game.

I had read about it before. His friend drove his car, lost control, and hit a tree. The football player was killed the day before the big game. The father, a minister, told the team to play, that his son would have wanted that. They did and scored 42 points, the same number the boy (Derrick) wore. And the next week, in the championship game at the Pontiac Silverdome (where Kyle and I saw Lowell beat Brother Rice,) Derrick's brother, Jim, wore the 42 jersey, led the team onto the field, and they again won—score: 42-13. As I read this article and the previous news items, I couldn't help but thinking about Kyle, also age 16 and a football player, also driving and sometimes too fast. It's snow-covered today and he wants to drive to the Shermans. "It's no big deal" to him, as it was for Derrick and his friend. And I think of Kenny, whose 34th birthday was two days ago. Judy bought a rock with a heart in it. She wrote in rainbow colors all the names of our family (Mom, Dad, Arnie, Judy, Leslie, Bruce, Kyle, Ilana, Marlee, and Karenna) surrounding the name (in larger black letters) of Kenny. We gave it to my parents on the 22nd (Sunday night) and they placed it on the tombstone Monday, in the aching cold, the shivering light of day—December 23, 2002.

In Memory of Kenny Goldman
2002

Sometimes we forget
The faded dreams
That can never be,
A life that disappeared,
Your life begun on an
Ice-drenched December
Night; after a Tigers' game,
Ended, less than a mile
From home, twenty
Heart-wrenching years

Ago. We imagine the
Soul of your voice again,
Chanting your Bar Mitzvah
Prayers, the joy of your
Lingering laugh. As we drift
Through the photo album,
The collage of your silent
Faces seem so out of focus
In this fog of disbelief.
Now our dreams are prayers

Of you hovering around us,
Keeping us safe and believing.
We imagine your faded shots
On the cracked pavement, each
A silent swish, and can see you
Gliding above the boys and girls
Running the court in a league
Named in your honor, guiding
Them to grow, to never stop,
To savor their lives.

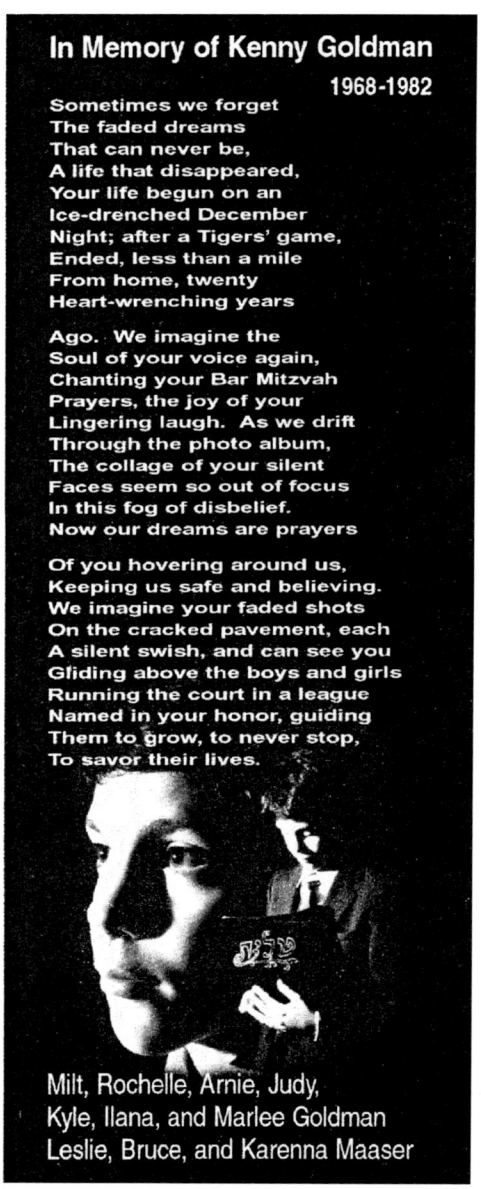

In Memory of Kenny Goldman
1968-1982

Sometimes we forget
The faded dreams
That can never be,
A life that disappeared,
Your life begun on an
Ice-drenched December
Night; after a Tigers' game,
Ended, less than a mile
From home, twenty
Heart-wrenching years

Ago. We imagine the
Soul of your voice again,
Chanting your Bar Mitzvah
Prayers, the joy of your
Lingering laugh. As we drift
Through the photo album,
The collage of your silent
Faces seem so out of focus
In this fog of disbelief.
Now our dreams are prayers

Of you hovering around us,
Keeping us safe and believing.
We imagine your faded shots
On the cracked pavement, each
A silent swish, and can see you
Gliding above the boys and girls
Running the court in a league
Named in your honor, guiding
Them to grow, to never stop,
To savor their lives.

Milt, Rochelle, Arnie, Judy,
Kyle, Ilana, and Marlee Goldman
Leslie, Bruce, and Karenna Maaser

Published in the *Detroit Jewish News*, July 2002

the dead come crawling
2004

the dead come crawling
in the middle of sleep
from the hotels of iraq
the michigan soldiers left
forlorn in a far away world
from the parched soil of gaza
the bombed out bodies
of kids in jerusalem
from the gethsemane gardens
with the spilled blood of
jesus from the new dawn
of the dead and its tattered
bodies ripped apart
coming at me coming
they keep coming at me
the senior from harrison
high hung in his room
seven years to the day
his brother hung himself
he keeps staring at me
with those vacant eyes
the eyes of the lost
in gaza in jerusalem
in iraq while i sleep
i cannot sleep
while the dead come
crawling come crawling
over my tired
live body

Tumor
2004

I was deaf
In my left ear
For a week
And a half,
A dull buzz pulsing
Through my head.

I couldn't hear
Anyone speak
On the left side,
Turning my head
To comprehend what
They were trying to tell me.

Everything in mono
A stereo with one
Speaker, I couldn't hear
The lovely sounds
Of Mahler's strings,
Just the dull roar

Of the beat, beat, beat
Of the bass drum
Of the Radiohead songs
On my newest CD.
I was afraid
I was losing

It, the hearing
On the left the first
To go, like Rush
Who'd lost both sides

And couldn't hear
Callers on his radio show.

Tests and more tests
Run at the ear doctor:
Not fluid, no virus,
No infections or mucus.
"It can turn off and then
On again like a faucet.

So we have to rule out
A tumor," the Doctor said
And sent me to Beaumont
For an MRI at 5:30am the
Next Friday in a dark cold
Tunnel of shrieking sounds.

Before the appointment
My hearing started again,
Slowly returning
Over two long days in Dennison,
Ohio like ice melting
Imperceptibly into water.

I was no longer
Worried, the chances of
Tumor slim, said the doctor,
And feeling the joy of hearing
In surround sound. I seemed
Invulnerable, fearless.

The test came back.
A CD only read by doctors
Revealed a tumor four
Millimeters long, an acoustic

Neuroma he called it, "certainly
The cause of my deafness."

Relatively safe to remove
Was the good news from the doctor,
To go through the base
Of the skull, to extract,
So the growing would stop
Against the border of my brain.

The bad news: Surgery
Was long, six to eight
Hours and would "definitely
Cause complete deafness
In my left ear, a loss
Of balance as well on that side.

Besides, a small chance
Of facial paralysis, two months
Of recovery, he warned,
And a possible loss of taste,
And headaches. It was easy
To decide to "watch and wait,"

See how fast the tumor'd grow.
So now, it grows inside
My head, slowly, without
Warning and will have to
"come out, soon or later,
the sooner the better."

Now I can hear Ilana's
Melodic songs in concert,
XM radio's 100 stations,
George Winston's quiet piano,

"The Planets" by Holst.
The Godfather's haunting melodies,

The whisper of my wife
On the right side in bed.
I can hear the pulse of everything
In ten speaker sound
From the honks of traffic
To the quiet hush of the fan.

So I wait and wait
And pray this tumor
Next to my brain stays
Still, small and stable,
Or better still shrinks
To the nothingness it was.

Tax Season
2004

I dedicated myself this year to do our taxes early, wading through our check books, donations, expenses, last year's statements, and all of our investment accounts. I got them together and sent what I had to my accountant in Chicago to coagulate together. Hopefully, we will be given a nice refund from the US and Michigan, at least enough money to pay the bills we owe.

Investment accounts? Did I say investments? This year, Bush and the Republican controlled Congress changed the tax laws, supposedly giving the middle class and "well-to-do" people more of their money back. Where is it? Where did it go? Dividends were reduced to 15, or was it 20%? Capital gain taxes were reduced if you hold it for x number of years. All I know for sure is that it's still confusing, even for accountants.

Investments? We have to calculate everything we've bought and sold, sold and bought, funds, stocks, bonds, everything. This brings back vividly the financial nightmare of the last four years. I get to relive (with millions of others) when we bought individual stocks which for us was 1999, near the end of the "bubble." I get to see again how much money disappeared from our accounts. Stocks we should have kept like Fortune Brands, Target, and Teva have doubled or tripled since we sold. Unfortunately, most stocks we held onto plunged headlong into the toilet. I get to see them again: Samsonite, Synergy Brands, Extreme Networks, Perfumania, Hasbro, Cisco, Xybernaut, Netro, Info Space, Vitesse Semiconductor, Quest, Priceline.com, JDS Uniphase, and everyone's favorite, MCI. We sold all of them at some point or another and lost money on all of them, a little on some, a substantial amount on others. I still get legal documents asking me to join thousands of others in class lawsuits against these companies, so we can give these lawyers the winnings we lost. I decline then and now. Why? Because it was MY Fault! No one forced me to buy. I was caught up in tech stock mania and pummeled in the downdraft.

I just finished the book, *American Sucker*, written by David Denby, the film critic of the New Yorker, and his similar experience from 1999 to 2003 when he tried to make a million dollars in the stock market to keep his New York apartment while going through a divorce. Instead, he literally lost a million dollars in stock value. I know that we lost thousands of dollars then. I try not to calculate or guess the grand total. The psychic nightmare I went through in 2000 through 2002, extending the role of bread winner of my family and trying to grow the pot of future dollars after my wife gave up on stock investing, is a journey I still try to forget. I thought I was well read on the market and knew what I was doing. I was wrong!

My father's friend, Hal, blew his brains out with a gun a few months ago on the floor of his large suburban home. He had lost virtually all of his money and his entire estate, leaving his wife and family with only a house and a little life insurance and a mountain of debt. After he left the advertising business in 1999, he became a full time day trader. He had done all of his day trading secretly, never telling anyone what he gained or what he lost or how much debt he had eventually gotten into. He suffered through the shame of losses and instead of sharing the pain and asking for help, he ended it all. He wrote in his final note that he thought it was best that way.

After going to the funeral, I felt that I understood the depth of despair that he went through. If the amounts of money I lost were greater and if I kept going the way I was going in 2000, I might have ended the same way. But I fought through worry and despair of dark market drops and never lost my will. I am not a gambler at heart because I hate to lose money a lot more than I like winning. That's what keeps me away from lotteries and casinos now. In the early eighties, I went through a summer of horse racing when I went to the track every night, betting my friend's money and my own. After weeks of losing every night, I finally gave up. I felt like a desperate loser and it hurt. Stock picking felt a lot like picking horses and eventually after

I lost enough, I killed the greed inside me and started focusing on conservative, sensible non-emotional investing.

Goodbye, Hal, goodbye to all the money we could have kept, goodbye to the stupidity of the past. Now, I will focus on how much I gave to the government, some of which I might get back. But just think, if I could take the money that disappeared from my paycheck and put it down on UT Starcom (UTSI,) my favorite stock of the moment, a company that's growing astronomically with sales to China and other Asian countries, if I…

Apart
2004

his wife lies
on the other side of the earth
under the Pacific sun
touching her reddening toes
on the soft hot sand
she looks into the distance
beyond the clouds
and imagines what it would be
without the shackles of
sickness and the wariness
of friends babbling on
about their worlds
their outstanding children
drifting off to college
under their all-knowing eyes
she is wrapped
in the soft stitches of yarn
the drifting worries
melting away in the heat
and glare of the light

her husband sits alone
on the couch mesmerized
by the glare of the cathode rays
his girls asleep after a long
day with the usual routines
dance glass and gymnastics
getting them stuff to eat
keeping it neat for his wife
who when she gets off the plane
will be overwhelmed by the
tiredness of time changes

and laundry and reading mail
and calling friends and her sister
and mother and the endless
list of stuff to do

he thinks of his partner
and why they were apart
again and why they are always
apart or so it seems
he thinks of her feet
touching his on the warm
blanket of sand and imagines
her gentle voice tugging against his
and her hands on his back
the closeness of two
who in twenty years have spent
so much and so little time together
their twenty year anniversary
two months from now

he remembers that day when
they met for lunch
and he fell in love
with her words and voice
and her outstretched hands
touched his and how he
never went back to work
and how they went to a friend's pool
and were the only ones
there or so it felt
and how he imagined being
naked with her and living
next to her for the
rest of his life

she was and is still
his destiny and he is happy
that she can take time
to be herself and lie
in the Hawaii sun and be content
and happy and trust
that her girls are safe
and taken care of and that
her husband misses her badly
and wishes and prays
with all his soul
that one day they will
lie together in the pacific
sun hand to hand
body against body
soul touching soul so
in love husband and wife
so in love

Anniversary Song
2004

twenty years ago
at the good earth restaurant
we saw each other
for the first time
a blind date
a chance for something
beyond what we were
beyond the simple phone
conversations we had
a chance for a new life

we ate greens and something
healthy and forgettable
which was not true of our
meeting that lasted and
lasted as we saw your best
friend's family and decided
to go somewhere else
instead of back to work
which is where I was
supposed to be

so we decided to venture
to your Russian friend's pool
and lay out in the sun
and relax and talk and
let the slowness of the day
carry us away
how we got there I don't
remember like much
of the day I forgot in
the fogginess of memory

what I do remember
is the absolute
freedom of my fantasies
the rush of
exhilaration horniness
desire for something you
offered I'd never felt
the dream of love
finding someone
who could share me
my fears and loneliness
who could awaken in me
what I thought had died
with my brother

the knowledge
that love and life
could be entwined
that the sad solitude
of a meager life
could be gone
replaced with
love and hope
a dream for us
this endless dream

Six
Permanent

My First Love
2005

1
On the third of March
I phoned my once-best friend
And wished him on his birthday
Another forty-eight years before his end.

We talked about the Pistons;
Our lives in high school, for memory's sake,
How we called each other through the years
On our birthdays, give or take.

Then he mentioned before hanging up
That Sandy, our classmate friend, he'd heard
Had died of cancer in January
Or February; at least, that was the word.

My few shaken words on the phone
Felt hollow and bitter as I said,
I remembered how much she drank
And smoked. I wasn't shocked she was dead.

2
Dead,
dead of cancer.
A classmate of mine,
a friend, so young,
an old friend.
Twenty-five years before,
we met again, the first time
since high school
at our five year reunion
at the local pizzeria,

Corsi's Pizza
on 7 Mile Road.

Where did I see her first?
When did her eyes catch mine?
Where did I draw the courage?
She was pretty and smart,
thin with long flowing,
blonde hair running
down her back,
the back of her sweater,
the stark eyes staring
or so it seems now.

That first conversation,
the beer feeding
our fearful tongues,
the endless words
whipping through our bones,
How lost we both felt,
two souls knowing nothing
but the loss
of high school youth,
the emptiness of memory.

How we both still wrote
poetry about a world
that wasn't ours,
a world that felt like
an old joke, a joke
we didn't get, but here we were
though we'd hardly spoken
in high school, when
we knew we were smart,
she number one on the

school grade hit parade,
I was number four.

Both of us writers,
would-be poets
or so we imagined ourselves,
both wasting our lives
after high school
in meaningless jobs,
both washing ourselves
of our hopes and dreams.

3
After the reunion
we went steady
as if we were in high school again,
steady as we talked on the phone
and went out and thought
about each other every
waking moment
or so it seems now.
We dated and touched
and talked and drank and sat
on her mother's couch
and kissed and wrote
poetry to each other
and shared our old poems,
and she drove to my apartment
where we sat on my green couch
and watched TV, ate TV dinners
I cooked in the microwave
and we stared at the gas
fireplace that never died
as I stared into her eyes
trying to find the right
words that would keep us

together, keep us whole,
wondering how we ever
got so lucky, how we finally found
each other, how we found
our true soul mates
after 23 years of life.

Or so it seems now
in the dark fog of memory
that we'd go out at night and drink
and fall into each other's arms
without clothes, without
anything separating us except the dark
thoughts of intoxicated love
which I barely remember, I don't
remember what it felt like
to touch her, to feel
her warm skin against my skin,
I don't remember
Anything. All I can see
in this hazy blur of mind
is one night, the night
Lennon was shot and we stayed up,
watched TV, listened to the radio
all night, her body
in my arms, how we
listened to "Help," "Eleanor Rigby,"
"Imagine," and then we wept
and held each other and hardly slept
until the sunlight
lashed our faces.

4
When I called my friend
on his birthday, he told me
Sandy, the valedictorian

of our class, was dead.
She had died of cancer.
The Big C had taken her,
her long blonde hair,
her lungs, and eventually
her brain and heart.

As I grow old, my hair
thins, the paunch grows
larger, the face wrinkles,
the eyes darken with lines.
25 years before, we'd met
again, after our five year
high school reunion,
both sad, lonely, two
bitter poets sick
with the world.
And for a few months,
only a few months,
we found ourselves
in the company of love.
We shared our poems,
wrote one letter
after another, and loved.
When Lennon died,
she was in my arms
and I felt the world
had died and I was born
again in her welcoming arms.

5
The computer screen's light
washes my face, hundreds
of emails waiting for viewing,
for response. My life's
a day on the chair, another

after another, talking, reading,
processing words, endless words.
She once was my every word,
my breath, my thoughts. I felt only
what she sent me, her words,
the sorrow and the sweetness,
those piercing eyes, both of us on her
mother's couch, the lights
from the Christmas tree
bathing us in their
tempestuous glow.

Why does the world
make no sense? Where
does the heartache spread?
In '79, she wrote, "i put
at rest and resting, crawl
on fossil knees in skin of gauze
take me away in stillborn air
and sail beyond the planet's prayer."

Sandy's sailed beyond the planet's prayer
and waits...for what? Retribution,
forgiveness, for the everlasting
life we pray is there, somewhere
"in this great sparkle fairyplace
of silken silver nothingness?"

6
When she told me it was over,
I took it like a man,
silent, aching, wondering why
but angry anyways.
She took me to the Walled Lake bar
we'd hung out many midnights before
under the hanging fluorescent lights.

She told me it was for
the best, that it hurt
and she loved me
but it was the best, the best.

The remembrance of stumbling
on the broken pavement, sometime
in the winter, bleary-eyed, half
in the bag, half heartbroken and
hardened. How I drove home
I don't know, leaving my memories
at the bar, scampering back to my
Westland apartment, my roommate,
and my empty green couch.
The car's stereo blasted the Clash's
"Hateful" and "I'm Not Down"
all the way home.

She wrote in her poem,
"The Love Seeker,"
"there have been men
and let me say again
their eyes were kind
and they were decent people, still—
there was a space they could not fill
and i moved on
i left them standing
with confusion, rather sadly
and i hope they don't think badly of me
i am decent too."

7
Did she save me from
her manic moments of anger
and despair? Did she protect me
from this beautiful woman

who could pierce without thinking?
Or did Sandy spare herself from
this man who could turn
so weak and desperate,
almost pathetic?

She was tempestuous,
the skin her prison;
she just wanted to fly away
even then, in words, in the
endless sky of wonder,
wondering why the world
wasn't better, something
could be better, somewhere,
somewhere out there,
always the impetuous
dreamer, and me
the hopeless, unnecessary noose
around her neck.

8
18 months after the breakup,
my brother, Kenny, was crushed
in an accident in my father's car,
and Sandy came to the funeral.
She wrote me a letter, quoting
"People" by Yevtushenko.
"They perish. They cannot be brought back.
The secret worlds are not regenerated."
"In any man who dies there dies
With him his first snow
and kiss and fight."

"Sometime," she wrote, "I think
the measure of a person
isn't what they've got,

but what they've lost.
And what they've felt."
"I am with you," she ended. "I am
with you now, as you read this letter,
no matter where I am."

Small consolation then,
So much more now.
Sandy, you were so much more
Than decent.

9
Sandy, you wrote the poem
"wish" in the seventies,
asking the "black sky" to
"bring me someone
who will say carry on."
Sandy, I am asking you to
carry on now. I am asking
you to be here now and fly
amongst us, to visit those
you love and leave,
without saying goodbye.
Can you see us here and help?
Will we sense you and
wonder if you're our
"Prince of Airnow"
and say to ourselves,
Is that your hair, your voice,
Your "shadow's sigh?"

I am the "dreamer"
you wrote of "who will sail
in a boat a crescent of silver,"
wishing we could have stayed pen pals,
wishing my brother would have grown

up with me, wishing you could have met
my wife, wishing she never found your letters,
wishing she never threw them out,
wishing fear and jealousy became
the wish to meet you instead,
wishing you could have met my children
and loved them the way I do,
wishing you could have been happy
through the sad stark years of your thirties,
wishing you could have found your future
husband earlier and lived a few more
years together, wishing that tired ache
you felt was not cancer, was not the
devastation of tumors filling your body,
wishing your hair stayed flowing white,
wishing your dogs could still lick
your Florida sand-wrapped feet,
wishing you could have stayed warm and
protected, wishing I could have emailed you
just once on classmates.com and heard
your words, just once,
just one more time, wishing I could have
seen you one more time, just once
to say I'm sorry about everything
and thanked you for giving me
once upon a time the capacity
to love, wishing that what I told
your mother is true, that the whistle
she hears at night is you,
it's really you.

You wrote to me after Kenny died,
"bear what is unbearable,
love more than is possible,
forgive what is unforgiveable."
Sandy, I will try to live

your words. I pray that you
are protected, that the words
you once wrote are true now,
"I am with you now as you
read this letter, no matter where
I am." You once wrote,
"I want to know that clover
is a magic thing and lightning bugs
are little starspecks
in the night sky."
Sandy, I am looking
at the night sky now,
searching for starspecks,
bearing what is unbearable.

Crack
2005

The MLB 2005 All Star
Game's coming to Detroit,
Super Bowl 2006 next
in the middle of winter.
In the NBA Finals at the Palace,
you could see Eminem on the
big Screen raising his hands
when Chauncey twisted his body
for a lay-up. We almost won
a championship again for the
second straight year. We feel
good for a few moments in this
town called Detroit. Everyone
today's entitled to employee
discounts on GM, Ford, and Chrysler
cars and trucks. Just turn the TV on.
Lee Iacocca, 80 years old,
is pitching new Chrysler cars
at good old "employee pricing."
It feels like old glory days
again in the streets of Motown.

Let's not discuss Ford and
GM losing a billion last quarter,
owing billions to those who
stopped working years ago.
Don't talk about which Detroit
Schools are closing, how
Detroit streets crack, no money
left in the budget to fix them.
Forget about the city now
number eleven in the new census,

just behind San Jose. Skip the
front page of the Detroit *Free Press*,
the stories about the mayor, Kwame,
his wife's Cadillac SUV,
his mansion and bodyguards
paid by a city that's broke.
Keep quiet about the real
business in Detroit which still is
crack, heroin, and the latest drugs
sold by the new Dells of Detroit,
the gang leaders of Livernois
and John R, spreading
bullets and death all the way
from 8 Mile to Fort Street.

The company my dad worked for
and I do now, Hardware Sales
and Supply, lived in Detroit
from 1925 to 1978 before it moved to
the suburbs of Madison Heights,
then Livonia. I remember riding
the Grand River bus when I worked
in the summer, the pungent smell of
diesel fumes, the rats found upstairs,
the day someone stole the flag
off the flagpole, high over the flat roof,
next to the Wonder Bread plant. I can
smell the hot bread in the morning
mixed with odors of my dad's
cigarettes puffed all day
while he walked with a phone,
its 40 foot cord, checking stock
on the new GM keys,
the latest Master padlocks.

Hardware Sales and Wonder Bread
are now the Motor City Casino
where thousands of Detroiters
cash their weekly checks, bringing
their dreams, believing
they will be the next lucky millionaires,
believing they will finally leave
this decrepit city with the highest
unemployment rate in the country,
believing they will escape
the drive-by drug-war shootings,
the daily death of an innocent kid
in the wrong window, in the wrong
street at the wrong time, believing
they will be the lucky one
whose time has come who will
cash in and drive out of the
cracked streets to a place
any place that's better safer
any place other than Detroit.

Burnout
2005

Four bombs detonated
Today in London, so there's
Panic on TV and numbers listed
On the internet: 37 killed,
700 wounded. I can hardly
Move as I stare at the flat screen
Monitor. It's July 7th,
A vacation week for some.
I stare at papers on my desk,
558 pages of a customer's pricing,
The new details of "split order mods,"
Directions printed off my email.
On my desk are "steps to take in
Dealing with unacceptable behavior
By your best people." A four color
Flyer by a Houston competitor
Awaits my decisions. What products
Do we advertise against them?
Silver code locks, polished brass
Knob locks, and "Groovy" colored
Keys stare at me, awaiting something.

I close the door, press the
Do Not Disturb button on the phone,
And answer a few emails. I feel
Like the Wizard of IDN,
Coming out from behind my
Curtain-door a couple times a day.
I stare at the Personnel Review Forms
I promised to do last month and
A synopsis of *Banishing Burnout*
Sent to me last week with accompanying

CD. I just can't get past the first page.
I want to sit back, listen to CNBC
On XM and take a nap.
I look at all three kids' photos
On my desk and know
I have to make a living. What
Am I supposed to do?

I'm given the weekly batch of invoices
To review and turn the pages,
Giving my okay without looking
At line item details. When did
The excitement stop? When did
I lose what drove me for 27 years?
A car door opens outside and I
Look at my watch. It's almost noon,
Good, it's time for lunch.

Out of the Closet
2005

I dream of walking out,
Leaving the company I've
Lived at, lived with, worked for,
Managed. Out, just walking,
Gone through the front door,
A sad goodbye to the people
I've hired, worked with, known
For so many years, my friends,
My fellow employees, my loved
Ones. I dream of desertion,
Telling those I work for
That I can no longer live
In fear, in anger, taking orders
That are wrong, doing
What I don't believe in.
Goodbye to the new computer
System, the outdated territory
Restrictions, the pointless
Policies drummed up by lawyers.

I dream of starting new,
Coming out of the closet,
Beginning the right way,
Focused on the best security
Products sold by friendly
People at just the right prices.
I dream of being a leader
Again in an industry
Slowly dying, dream of
Having fun again, being
Innovative on the internet,
On the leading edge
Of what makes sense.

It's time to check my stocks
Online, to see if companies
I invest in have risen or fallen,
The S&P and NASDAQ at four year
Highs. My worries feel over
For a short, short time and
Then I think of Hal ,my father's friend,
Once a big-time ad exec at Campbell Ewald,
His glory years with Chevrolet,
How he got caught up
In the stock market "bubble"
Of the nineties and sat
In front of a screen after hours
Day trading, hitting it big
Or so we all thought
And he left Campbell or
They fired him but
He seemed happy, believing
He would do better on his own.

The Millennium arrived,
The NASDAQ hit 5000
And what once was big
Racing higher went down
The arrows shot downward
and Hal must have lost it almost
Lost it all yet kept going
Never saying a word to his wife
His friends like my father,
And he kept living the high life
In Wabeek, Bloomfield Hills,
Still went out to the Stage
And other restaurants,
Never admitting anything.
How he must have lost
The urge to go on or admit

Defeat, to tell his wife
It was all a lie, he was sorry.
Instead, he checked his
Life insurance papers, his
Estate, what was left of it,
Wrote a note and pulled the
Trigger aimed at his head,
the blood seeped out into the
Cracks of his hard wood floor.

I think of the stocks I owned
In 2000, MCI, Cisco, Quest, JDSU,
Nortel, Infospace, all of them
Dropping into the bare bones
Of what they once were. Now,
I look at the domain names
I've chosen for the future
Businesses I want to start,
All of them, staring at me
Because that's all I've done,
Got domain names and nothing else,
Peaceofmindproducts.com,
m-safe.com, locksafestore.com,
safesmartsimple.com,
simplesafesecurity.com, and
independentlock.com, all parts
of the American dream, Arnie G
The next great leader.
I know I can do it, I took
Over this company and built it
Tripling sales, profits,
People. I know I can build
My own company and get
Those I know and respect
To come work with me,

They'll follow me and we'll
Do things right, be the
Growth company in the industry,
With an internet site anyone
Can buy from, affiliated customers
Selling great security products
Through the eyes of the internet
Drop shipped from us,
The newest coolest high tech
Electronic products that will sell
Because they are new, innovative,
Because we will market them right,
Yes we will know our stuff
And have few restrictions, we will
Have fun and do it all right,
Work can be fun and rewarding
And joyful. Regrets, I want
No regrets, I want to look back
A few years from now
Sick with something, fearing death,
But knowing that I took
A chance and did what I could.
I went all the way.

Three weeks ago in the *Jewish News*
I found Lou's picture in the
Obit section, a member of our synagogue
Adat Shalom, I saw him every
Year on Yom Kippur in the
Back row, he was always friendly
When you saw him. I was told
He went bankrupt as he ran his used
Car store on Grand River, Farmington,
Went into heavy debt meaning
To pay it back, he would one day

Hit the winner and his brother-in-law,
My oldest friend, found him
A job at a used car lot
And sold him his life insurance,
And things looked stable until
He shot himself, they
Found him on the driveway,
The Insurance he bought to keep his wife
Going was not two years old yet,
Was therefore no good.
It was no good.

A little luck separates us
As I sit in disgust when our company
Declines but I follow policy and
Faithfully execute company commands
And convert to a computer system
I don't have faith in, keep costs
Down firing those I hire,
Following old-fashioned
Policies that worked fifteen years ago.
I watch with dread when stocks go down,
What I thought would work doesn't, what
I thought would be a winner isn't.
I don't tell my wife for fear of
Her disgust and telling me to stop
Gambling on our future
As she spends money daily at
Stores for the kids; we keep buying stuff,
More stuff we don't use, the basement filled
With junk to be sold on ebay,
Our credit cards used almost daily,
Our kids in private schools, our son
In Wharton, yet still wanting us
To set him up in a new venture

He's sure will win. The laws
Of supply and demand mean
Addiction to shopping, buying,
Throwing away, selling on ebay,
Buying on ebay. I can't tell her
What's in my heart, how I try to make
More and more for us, to grow
The "nest egg," to be smart,
To be strong, be the leader
My family, my company expects.

Instead, I look in the mirror
And see a fat, graying face
Filled with doubt, Hal and Lou,
Combined in one, the loner
Working to be the bread
Winner for his family
Filled with shame but still
With hope that one day
He will hit it big
He will be the big
Success he knows he can be.

One day you look into your eyes
Your soul and know you've had
Enough that all of it the money you owe
The getting up going out to make
A living to bring home what you're
Worth is no longer worth it
You succumb to the overwhelming
Sadness the hopelessness the fear
Realizing you're no good a loser
Not to be missed not a Dell
Or Davidson you know you'll
Never amount to anything

Great you can't tell anyone
Especially your wife who'll never
Understand who'll wonder why didn't
You just work like everyone else
Get a regular paycheck keep
The gold chain on with the
HDTV I Pods SUV's three
Bathrooms two dogs four cars
Two car garage two and a
Half baths hard wood floors
The chosen lot on the cul de sac
The landscaped lawn the deck
That needs staining the taxes
That rise every year health
Insurance statements car
Insurance bills Visa Amex
Discover MasterCard.
Unlike the commercial,
Nothing is priceless.

If the mediums are right
There's no way out.
Lou and Hal can see us still
And know they know
They abandoned the ones
They loved, left messes
For their families to wipe away,
Sacrificed themselves and
Their survivors. Did they
Escape or are they
Infinite prisoners
Of their own greed,
Their own personal hell?

I sit here staring
At the floor
In the basement
At the fear of
The future, the eventual
Deaths of those I love,
My own mortality
Staring at me as
I decide, what else
Can I decide
But to do nothing
Be nothing
To go forward
In this life
What should I do
With my life
But pray
Just pray?

Down
2005

What would I give to believe
like my brother-in-law Joel
that everything is possible
that no matter how far down
we are we can come back
we can always come back?

I think of him watching
another showing of *Wizard of Oz*
every single time it's on TV
another James Bond movie
and *Batman* the rerun or movies
doesn't matter which

He asks me once a day every day
when we're going to see *Batman
Begins* or how about *Charlie
and the Chocolate Factory*
and which Lions game we'll see
in November to celebrate his
48th birthday

He stays up every night
late watching TV doing his daily
exercise program his daily
schedule until he just can't stay up
anymore and finally falls asleep
only to doze off
on and off again
the next day every day
he's tired all day

He asks me if I can get him
another year of *ABC Soaps* and
Soap Opera Digest which he tears
pages from scatters over the couch
and floor every week every year
so he won't miss anything new
so he can crack the latest case
of *General Hospital All My
Children One Life to Live*

My mother-in-law asks me to help
to tell him I won't order
soap opera magazines if he doesn't
clean up all his clippings and
football schedules and daily sports
scores he listens to me always
welcomes me asks how I'm doing
and then how am I doing again
I his lone "buddy"

I can only smile and
think of him listening
to every Tigers game and thinking
they still have a chance to win it all
they still have a chance I think
of us together at the Lions game
when Reggie Brown was crippled
and Barry passed 2000 yards
and the Lions reached the playoffs

Or when he puts his favorite foods
together on the seder plate
and mashes them up with catsup mustard
turkey potatoes "bitter herbs" all of it

143

after he's read the four questions
in perfect staccato pronunciation
and laughs when he sings the
chorus of Dayeynu

I smile, not trying to imagine
how it felt for his parents
to bear their first child in 1957
with down syndrome an extra
chromosome number 21 and I can't
imagine that the average age
of death is forty-nine
is next year

What would I give to believe
like Joel that we're never down
that there's always a chance?
He is my Peter Pan
always looking forward
to another game
another win. When he and I
left a Lions game against Miami
in 2000, down
by three touchdowns
and a field goal
three minutes to go
all I could hear was heartbreak
in his voice as he begged me to
take him by the hand and
get us to my car fast
so he could hear us
make our comeback
to erase the impossible
lead to let us win
again just let us win

Groomsman
2005

I
In the scattered junk of the
basement I try to bring your spirit
back to life listening to a CD
The Killers Jimmy Eat World
and Green Day burned from my
I Tunes library you could
have shared with me
if you were still here.

I want to believe Rebecca and
Jody the mediums who tell me
all the spirits are around me
when I speak on the phone
I want to believe the M they say
might be you is really you Mike
that it's not some two-bit con
job ghost magician's trick.

My spirit's spinning in the
wind of my brain the perpetual
torment of losing a close cousin
friends aunts uncles and the
brother who was your friend too
the one closest in age to you
who went to a California beach
soaking up the sun next to you

Once upon a time in this Kodak
photo that really wasn't long
ago I want to believe that you
and Kenny and my Aunt not your
mom Shirley and my Uncle

Sid are preparing a party for me
when I arrive that God or something's
telling you it's okay everything's okay.

II
I have tried to forget the old times
at Woodcrest when we'd waste our time
drinking watching movies
The Godfather again under the Godfather
poster over the fireplace *Diner
Stripes Animal House SCTV*
and how we ended the night
at the Bone Yard eating a slab
of ribs a half chicken that huge
plate of greasy flat fries

How we'd end up back at the
apartment in the hot tub the
indoor-outdoor pool in the middle
of winter the blowing snow
falling on our bare skin
and we'd sip our beers and talk
about your Uncle Milt and your
Dad Morey and how much you
idolized them both and wanted
to believe you were just like them.

When I got married we didn't
talk much more or drink or discuss
movies we went our own ways
you going to New Orleans to work
for Acme our sister company and
meeting your first girlfriend and
I having my first child and busy
with the day to day of married life

still you'd stood up at my wedding
my good-looking single groomsman.

I don't know the details about why
they let you go and I didn't want to
know why you broke up and moved
back home and sold Zep chemicals
how much you "partied" and got
wasted almost every day and I didn't
want to question my crazy cousin
who lived life the way you wanted
wearing your sunglasses inside not
letting us see your bloodshot eyes

The pain they held as you stammered
in mumbling something at every
party where I saw you I was just glad
to see you to talk just briefly about
old times TV shows both of us
liked *Taxi Cheers Seinfeld* and you'd
talk with love about our dads
and your cousin Kenny you were
one of few who would mention
how "special" he was my only brother.

And I didn't want to know much
about the day your brothers broke into
your house and found you dead
on the floor the pungent smell of
Zep chemicals everywhere you'd been
sick with a cold the flu and wouldn't
see a doctor wouldn't drink or eat
wouldn't open the door or ask
for help wouldn't ask for help
Why didn't you ask for help?

III
At the funeral we wondered why
what happened was it stubbornness
desperation or did you just not care
any more? Your dad stood proud
telling us how good you looked as he
lived through his last year of
dementia not knowing what was going
on spared the agony of the present

The questions your mother and brothers
still ask themselves today when they
look at the picture of their handsome
son smiling brother the one who had
the potential to be so much more
yet maybe in the darkness of your
small suburban house you laughed
knowing you were ending it your way

I want to believe you did it like Frank
your way that you are like Michael
Corleone on the other side the one who
looks out for the family I want
to believe that when your brother went
out boating in the middle of the day
depressed distraught that it was you
who brought him there to see the young

Girl who was drowning I want to believe
like your brother Fred that you brought
him there to save her call for help
to bring the joyful tears you brought
to her parents I want to believe that you
were not forsaken and that your soul
is here in the ever-present sky
still my friend my groomsman.

Outlive Me
2005

As I tiptoe from bedroom to bedroom
unable to sleep, I move closer
to my children's faces,
their ears cuddling the pillows,
deep into their death-defying dreams.
their breathing stops and starts,
the faint snoring of their hard-working
chests rising and falling inward,
their breaths rhythmically slowing.

My oldest daughter is taking her
road test Saturday to get her license,
my son is due to graduate Wharton in
less than three years and my youngest
daughter is in the fifth day of her
second period. She told me with
a voice of sadness
that she can't go swimming
in "papa's pool." I want to tickle
her armpits and wake her, let us
listen to our iPod Shuffles
together and forget that she
will be Bat Mitzvah'd in two years.

Not even eleven years ago
she escaped from my wife's womb,
her screams bursting in the hospital
room, the blood covering her eyelids.
I thanked everyone then, God
Mother Nature my wife the nurses
for this monumental moment,
this third and last miracle
of my life. I pull up a chair

and gently kiss her cheek.
I wait and wait, thinking of the
Coldplay song Ilana loves,
"Don't panic" which repeats and repeats
the words, "We live in a beautiful
world." I can't stop hearing it
and start singing in the faintest of breaths.

Marlee starts to stir, her eyelids
fluttering, as if she could feel me
hovering over her,
as if she could hear my prayer
as loud as I'm thinking it:
Outlive Me,
Outlive Me.

My daughter, Marlee

Permanent
JULY 21, 2005

It's "google" day today,
the day they announce earnings.
Kyle's excited, his stock,
now at 313, is rising.
Kenny would have liked
the company, would have
liked searching on a screen,
one split second after another,
searching for anything,

23 years now
since his last breath,
his last day alive,
the midnight he fell
asleep for the last time,
the last time.

I drive alone to
Machpelah Cemetery,
alone, my wife in pain,
an ice pack under
her back, moving back
and forth, sideways
on the living room couch.
I wave goodbye and look
for the blue yarmulke
that reads, "Bat Mitzvah
of Ilana Goldman,
August 25, 2001."

As I drive toward Woodward,
the only song I hear is
Coldplay's "What If,"

my head fog like, the
rain finally stopped, and
when I enter the grounds,
no cars are here, just
some men with weed
whackers cutting
around the stones.

Approaching Sec. 23,
Row 9, I look for a rock
to put on his stone,
trying to remember the
Mourner's Kaddish,
as I stare below at,
"Forever In Our Hearts
KENNETH GOLDMAN
Beloved Son & Brother
Dec. 23, 1968—July 21, 1982."

I remember the hours
it took to write the
three lines underneath,
creating them, changing
the words, erasing them
again and again and
finally settling on
YOUR FLAME BURNED SO BRIEFLY
BUT OUR LOVE LIVES AND WILL COVER
YOU, KENNY, IN THE LONG DARK NIGHT.

The sun is pounding
against my head,
against the stone
and its words, words
so permanent, etched

forever into gray rock,
these words that once
meant so much
and so little.

My grandmother, Anna, and her Mother, Golda, early 1930's.

Namesake
AUGUST 18, 2005

I
Another sorrowful day passes
for Cindy Sheehan, a mom waiting
in the dry heat of Texas to see
President Bush and talk about her son
shot down dead in Iraq. I can only
wait at my work desk staring
at the copied photo of my grandmother,
Anna, staring at a camera sometime
in the thirties, her mother
at her side. There is no smile.
I can feel the haunted stare
Down my neck.

Every half hour, a girl on CNBC
sings "happy birthday" to Google
turning one today as a publicly traded
company. I click the mouse to google
Anna Sherman Goldman of Michigan,
to discover her lost life.
Pages scroll but nothing comes close.

What do I know of the person who
mothered my father, whom I was named
after. A three-year old girl who came here
from Lithuania with her mother Golda,
her father Louis, both orthodox Jews.
The oldest of seven children. During
the First World War, she married another
immigrant, Neyman Goldman, who left
Russia at ten. They married,

had seven children who lived,
three who died.

At my lunch break, I keep driving
all the way to 8 Mile Road,
all the way to Woodward,
past the strip clubs, the adult book
stores, past the man sleeping on a chair
at the corner of 8 and Woodward,
bearing a sign that says, "Homeless veteran.
Got screwed. Need help." The light
is green as I pass and turn around
while the Woodward Dream Cruise
warms up for Saturday; passing on my right
some old convertibles super-charged,
waiting to relive the glory of Detroit past.

I wander down the aisles of the cemetery
again, four weeks since the last time
I visited this garden of the dead,
to view the monuments honoring
the lost and forgotten ones, our
indelible past. I cannot remember
where my grandmother's tombstone lies.
And so my walk begins from one
section to another. I wish I could google
her location on my cell phone and
magically go to her place of rest.

It's unbearably humid, the sweat
running down my neck. I go to where
I know, my brother's grave, now
covered with "perpetual" flowers,
our message erased by pink and green.

I pass Anna's youngest sister, Jean,
who I remember as the kindest person
I knew, and next to her, Jack her husband.
I pass her sister, Edith, and my Uncle Irving.
How many more I don't even know,
names familiar and names I forgot.

But where are my grandparents?
Where is Uncle Sid? Turning to the front
of Machpelah, I see an office
I've never known and open the door slowly.
I ask the lone woman if she has a list of the dead
and their locations. She does and writes where
Sid and my grandparents reside; on a map
she marks each section, row, and lot.
My uncle is first, in the "Memorial Garden."
I pay my respects and head to my mother's
parents Sam and Ida, who died when I was
nine and fourteen. Sam owned a drugstore,
had a nervous breakdown in his fifties.
He was heavy and bald and
had a heart attack at 59.
I think I have his genes.

I turn to the back and head to Section 22,
to the left of my brother, down the same row.
My Zadeh died less than nine months
after Kenny, on the birthday of his daughter,
Sylvia, three years older than my dad.
Zadeh was never told of the accident,
but I always believed
he knew. His mind was deteriorating
but he knew. I watch him in my
mind's eye slicing the bread at

Kenny's Bar Mitzvah,
Kenny smiling by his side.

I can stay for just a minute
and turn to the left to Section 18,
row 4, lot 15 at the very left
of the cemetery. I still can't find
my grandmother, walking row to row,
searching for her stone, counting
every marker, telling myself
no matter what I will find her,
I've been here over an hour
In the scorching heat, I will
find her, I will find her.
And finally, right in front of
my eyes, her tall tombstone stands,
In Memory of Anna Goldman,
Loving Wife and Mother,
December 23, 1891-
March 5, 1955.

II
Why didn't I know you were born
on the same day as your grandchild
Kenny whom you also never knew?
Was I told and forgot? I can only stare
at the stone that bears your name.
I can only imagine what my father
says of you, how unhappy you were.
He says to look at your picture and
understand what you felt day by day,
bearing and raising seven children,
feeding them, keeping kosher
in the depression, your husband,

a tyrant to you and your kids,
coming home late from work
night after night, so little money,
so little time. He tells me you'd
run from the house screaming,
in your solitary pain. How did you
cope with Sid's rheumatic fever,
my dad's double pneumonia,
the constant bouts of flu? I can't imagine
what you felt when your two
little babies, Lillian and Jeanette,
died before their first birthdays.

When I wake in the middle of night,
struck with the terror of death,
am I feeling you? When I kneel
down on the ground in tears,
am I lost in your dread?
My father tells me in 1939,
when he was nine, you suffered
your last nervous breakdown.
You were confined to Eloise
till the end of your life.
Sixteen years in solitude,
a few glimpses of your
children visiting their
"mentally ill" mother.

I am so sorry
for not knowing,
sorry for not caring.
I want you to know
if you can ever
hear me that I am proud

to carry your name,
proud to be your grandchild.
On my brother's birthday,
I will also celebrate
the day you were born
and fell in love with my Zadeh
and brought seven children
into the world to bear
sixteen more, including
my sister, brother, and me.

I will be
your namesake
as long as I
am alive
will never forget you
for the remaining
gift
of my life.